Blood & Honey

The Secret Herstory of Women
South Slavic Women's Experiences
in a World of Modern-day Territorial Warfare;
How daughters, mothers, and grandmothers
heal their communities and circumvent
another century of wars

By

Danica Anderson PhD

Danica Anderson

Artists:
Connie Simpson. Back Cover and images on pages: 30, 38, 48, 86, 98, 130
Erin Hilleary. Front Cover and images on pages: 14, 41, 56, 64, 77, 78, 92, 95, 108, 116, 124
Danica Anderson page: 72

ISBN 978-0-9886891-4-5

Olympia WA, 98516 USA
info@kolocollaboration.org
www.kolocollaboration.org
www.cookingwithbloodandhoney.com

Design by www.ipublicidades.com

Table of Contents

Klagenfurt
Austria
Maribor
Nagykanizа
Kaposvar
Hungary
Celje
Kranj
Varazdin
Koprivnica
Pecs
jana
Slovenia
Novo Mesto
Zagreb
Bjelovar
Virovitica
Ivanic- Grad
Drava
Kocevje
Uljanik
Kupa
Karlovac
Sisak
Pakrac
Nasice
Osijek
Sava
Slavonska Pozega
Rijeka
Glina
Croatia
Omisalj
Slavonski Brod
Slunj
Bosanski Novi
Bosanski Brod
Senj
Prijedor
Derventa
Krk
Cres
Otocac
Bosanska Krupa
Bihac
Banja Luka
Pag
Gospic
Udbina
Bosanski Petrovac
Karlobag
Jajce
Bosnia and Herzeg
Zenica
Zadar
Dugi Otok
Kain
Livno
Sara
Bosna
Sibenik
Sinj
Adriatic Sea
Split
Brac
Mostar
Hvar
Gacko
Ploce
Poluotok Peljesac
Korcula
Ston
Mijet
Trebinje
Dubrovnik

Introduction

Translated from Serbo-Croatian to English, the word Balkan means "blood and honey" (Bal means honey, kan means blood).

The Balkan War of the 1990s has become a popular reference to the horrors of war. The media bombards us with the babushka-swathed images of South Slavic Bosnian, Muslim, Serbian, and Romano women. These mother-daughter images are more decorative than alive in the minds of viewers, the gallery of images connecting the Balkan War to the World Wars I and II. Rather than displaying each photograph beside the next on the museum wall, each could be layered upon the other, merging into one grandmother who represents the turmoil of the twentieth century. "Grandmother 1912" would become the outline for "Grandmother 1994."

At times, it seems as if I, alone, acknowledge the fact that three generations of grandmothers faced such similar horrific life experiences. This atrocity is certainly not at the forefront of contemporary discussion on women's issues and political affairs. Yet, the thousands of women whose traumatic pasts have trickled down into their daughters' and their daughters' daughters' lives must not be ignored—nor forgotten.

This book will divulge how trauma erases the female-based community and culture that once forged an immense socio-psychological peaceful collective in Neolithic and Paleolithic Europe. In the face of modern day territorial warfare, South Slavic women possess a powerful, yet often neglected, tool that has the potential to heal grief-stricken communities around the world. The women's stories represent more than the pale slips of paper found in interdisciplinary works of research; they are undervalued narratives, which many academic and medical experts consider to be nothing more than first-person accounts that offer little to the empirical community. However, I have experienced the psychosomatic healing that exudes from the women's kolo rituals, an oral memory tradition science of ancient round dancing and other practices, that is not easily captured by traditional empirical methods.

Essentially, Blood & Honey is the secret history of women surviving masculine domination and the perpetrators' attempts to eradicate female collectives. I explore pseudo-clinical approaches to trauma treatment, like the classic use of the couch or the desperate dependence on an empirical text, through which clinician's often thumb in search of the perfect approach. Yet, as shown by both statistics and women's narratives, such modern courses of treatment fail to awaken and heal the horrific trauma experienced by the three generations. But the very herstory of these women offers a healing practice that has, to this point, been overlooked: the kolo.

My thirst to discover the seamless intergenerational transmission of violence led to a startling, yet unifying, hypothesis: my experiences are shared with you, your mothers, your daughters, and all mothers and daughters who were and will be. Following the paths and patterns of South Slavic female practices has linked my childhood places of intergenerational trauma to a parallel trajectory: I share a path in life with Bosnian women who are war crimes survivors, but also with women worldwide, such as my sisters in Africa and Asia. My heavy heart knows that violence against women is a silent yet massive collaborative war. Despite the relentless attacks on our sisterhood, women around the world continue to practice mothering, nurturing, and caregiving practices, thereby etching culture into future generations and surviving— and sometimes thriving— as the daughters of our "Moist Mother Earth," as the South Slavs call her.

The practices of the Bosnian-Herzegovinian Muslim women taught me that by interrupting intergenerational violence, women can heal their own communities, circumventing another century of wars. I witnessed the effects of the

▲ Boyd Miller

Serbian intergenerational trauma, and my focus became transfixed on identifying the healing practices of the community. I turned to the indigenous South Slavic practice of the kolo, a round dance that represent the wheel of life. After a decade of work with female war survivors, I found their strength and healing embedded in the first-person stories shared by daughters, mothers, and grandmothers who were pried from the hermetically sealed coffins of their loved ones. Intuitive and loving, these women address the imbalance induced by their twisted Slavic kinesthesia by participating in ancient kolo practices.

The kolo is a circular folk dance whose origins extend into the Mesolithic era and is still practiced throughout most of Eastern Europe and Russia. I lived and breathed the South Slavic kolo practices of applied kinesiology, where body movements are interconnected with matter and all living relations and where memories are transgenerational-shaping genetic materials as rituals and traditions. I searched deeper and engaged with the circles, listening and feeling as the narratives moved the collective into healing harmony. I came to understand that the kolo is story told through movement and memories that offers the healing of trauma and forges peaceful communities.

I am not sure I will ever know the truth of how my mother had survived the Jasenovac concentration camp.

I have tried to visualize my mother in Yugoslavia during WWII, with its smoking chimney stacks stinking of roasted human flesh. Jasenovac concentration camp, erected in August of 1941, had the largest number of ethnic Serb victims, about half of the nearly 100,000 men, women, and children who perished in the sweet-smelling chambers[1].

Jasenovac Brick Ovens

Born a Serbian-American daughter, I discovered that the gut-wrenching smell from the chimney stacks had drifted across the generations; I inherited that traumatic experience with its accompanying South Slavic earthly landscapes and fields that smoking chimneys once towered over. Some have suggested that every six minutes we breathe an atom of air that was once breathed by our ancestors[2].

---

1 Visit the official homepage of the Jasenovac Memorial Site: http://www.jusp-jasenovac.hr

2 "In *The Sacred Balance*, Suzuki quotes Shapley as saying that 'Your next breath will contain more than 400,000 of the argon atoms that Ghandi breathed in his long life. Argon atoms are here from the conversations at the Last Supper, from the arguments of diplomats at Yalta, and from the recitations of the classic poets.' And from the exhalations of the dinosaurs, the whales and the sabre-toothed tigers. Air, says Suzuki, is 'a matrix that joins all life together,' past and future as well as present. We inhale our ancestors and exhale into the lungs of our children. Furthermore, by befouling the air - and the water, and the earth - we very literally befoul ourselves."

SD Cam. (2011, March 20). The most important idea in the world [Web log post]. The green interview. Retrieved from http://www.thegreeninterview.com/blog/most-important-idea-world-sunday-column-march-20-2011

You see, experiences of trauma are not simply memories; rather, these experiences are traumatic encounters that trigger the endless repetition of fear, flight, and intergenerational violence.

As a child, I could not help my mother nor break her free from her traumatized silence. I eventually took on the punitive role of the scapegoat in my dysfunctional family. My childhood was a blur of acutely disturbing, raw, and unfiltered child abuse. But in moments of seeking the unsaid truth, I pursued the progression from scapegoat to student of intensified learning in the cycle of intergenerational trauma.

The intensified learning is how I move through the cultural femicide, the mass murder of her life experiences not just her body. The precious oral memory traditions encompassing all women's stories not just my mother's life experiences. You see my mother's life experiences already has happened to us all. Intergenerational trauma perpetuates the mass murder of women's lives and stories, the very voices that has been known to heal the world of violence we live in.

I did not enjoy the lesson plan nor embrace the knowledge of my mother's painful memories. But I understood why my mother had avoided being reviled by the past. She hid behind the silence that blinds us, her veil of denial and avoidance. The nature of collective memories, of a whole tribe of women surviving decades of wars and violence, is especially cruel. The cruelty lies in the same minuscule utterance encased by walls of shame and the same silence that blinds us and binds us to the custody of our fathers, brothers, and husbands—the men who promise to protect us, yet whose protection only generates more violence in a seemingly endless cycle of masculine domination.

My mother's refusal to speak of her incarceration in the concentration camp was further convoluted by her failure to mention my maternal Great Uncle Marko. When I eventually learned of her experiences and those of my maternal great uncle, I was struck by an inability to relate to my mother's silence—a familiar struggle I had faced as a young mother when I could not fathom why my mother had refused to hold my infant children. When Uncle Marko came to town, it all became clear.

I have always known that my shadow side has been unable to reason with women's acquiescence to mindless conformity. It's a matter of holding memories sacred for their shape shifting of our DNA. Thus, when a woman shuns a past memory, she shuns her own children—her future—that which can heal the horrific painful memories by forging new memories capable of healing wounds. Along with my realizations, I came to learn that cruel memories are traumatic experiences that produce behavioral symptoms as a result of our fight or flight neurological processes[3].

Zorka Medic Borkovich right side, end of bench in 1972, Banja Luka Bosnia

I now realize that Uncle Marko was an unlikely archeologist specializing in the exhumation of long-buried realities. Uncle Marko was tall, with chiseled cheeks that were familiar from an old photograph of him and his father that I remembered vividly from my young childhood. He wore spectacles that I would think only archeologists would wear. Like the practice of digging up remnants of artifacts and grave goods interred with ancient people, Marko brought my mother's true existence to light. Hailing from Calgary, Manitoba, in Canada, Uncle Marko finally answered my questions about how my mother had survived the concentration camp.

He flew down to Arizona to see my mother and to meet my children and me. Imagine my surprise, along with a huge shock, when my great Uncle Marko arrived on my doorstep. I was perplexed, given that my immigrant parents had previously sworn there were no blood relatives in North America, that they all lived in Yugoslavia—that is, if they had survived the war.

During his visit, Uncle Marko shared stories with me, but that which piqued my interest the most was uttered in only a few words. He recalled my mother's duty of "... cleaning the ovens for a potato." As a daughter who had witnessed her mother struggle with the past, I was good at digging into traumatic emotional graves. What my mother had done in the concentration camp shocked and revolted me. I heard from his few sentences enough horror to explain why she had refused my own infants.

I remember thinking that I had some secret skill of motherhood for my infants because of my mother's refusal to cradle babies. Or worse yet, that I

3 "When the child is unable to link ongoing, self-defeating, disruptive behavior to trauma experience, the underlying fear persists. This interferes with the child's ability to modulate emotions either through altering the persistence of refractory, self-limiting cognitive schema or the inability to use new experience to develop and grow. The flexibility of children to discriminate new information may be lost; the children are either numb to new information or hyperalert and perceive danger." (p. 16)

Burgess, A. W., Harman, C. R., & Clements, P. T. (1995, March). Biology of memory and childhood trauma. *Journal of Psychosocial Nursing and Mental Health Services, 33*(3), 16-26.

was not cradled because I failed to measure up in my mother's eyes. But instead I learned from my maternal Uncle Marko that her hesitancy came from a lethal economic exchange, the capitalism and consumerism that is indoctrinated into everyone as being the democratic way. When Uncle Marko explained the genocidal, and even gynocidal, events that shaped my mother, I realized that I had been exposed to the vast array of subtle hostilities and microinequities that range from not just my Uncle Marko, but from many males' looks, gestures, and backhanded compliments, like Great job! You are living proof that women really do have technical minds! They might as well add, And you're willing to kill babies for a potato.

Gynocide, the systematic destruction of women, isn't just a matter of equal opportunity; it often means a better bottom line for those in power. Gynocide is the mass murder of all life and things feminine that became for my mother a mode of economic exchange to be endured while interned in a concentration camp. For her, the economic exchange for WWII concentration camp survivorship was a potato that she earned for cleaning the ovens into which she had also been forced to throw babies to their deaths. It is said that she was lucky that she was young, with a wide Slavic body that could be a beast of burden for the menial earth-shattering labor required to fuel the holocaust.

My mother never confirmed the name of the concentration camp that held her to me. I learned later, after her Death in 2014, that she told my niece she was held in the worst concentration camp in former Yugoslavia, Croatia—the Jasenovac camp. Although I closely resemble my maternal Aunt Danica, who I had met in Bosnia in 1977, I often wonder if my mother's choice to name me Danica

Woman feeding the pigeons Bascarsija, (marketplace), Sarajevo

was in fact her attempt to address the horror of throwing infants into the ovens and then surviving to have her own child. I never knew of existence of my maternal aunt until then as if my mother threw her away.

It seems my lesson plan in life deems it necessary for me to see the horrors of my childhood as transpersonal educators. Every revealed truth forced me to learn how to manage vast collective memory dynamics. But the first steps were painfully deficient. I felt unprepared as a child and as a young mother to deal with the immensity of intergenerational memories of trauma.

I felt the immense burdens of my mother and father transferred directly to my heart. I acknowledged that I was given the truth silently, as if by an invisible intravenous tube, coursing into my veins through my mother's blood. I had no recourse as a daughter of Serb immigrants but to survey the unsaid truth and see it never forgiven. I ask, is it possible to forgive the unforgiven?

The fear is that if the truth is spoken then gossip, paranoia, and blame, the arsenal of trauma, will bury the truth alive in dead hearts. Truth-tellers fear that their words will be twisted into something even more horrible than the truth, simply because people cannot bear the actual reality, and then there will be no way to un-speak those words. Words, when spoken from the truth of her realities, carry a shadow; each word is a soul.

My childhood was like many other universal childhoods: embroiled in violence, including brutality that escalated into gynocides, war, and a form of torture called marriage that is merely a coupling of two strangers teeming with domestic violence, sexual assault, and child abuse. This experience of marriage has existed for many generations. My decades of work across the globe support, if nothing else, my experiences as a gatherer of a global collective trauma for the females of our species.

Observing my mother, I see that her trauma experiences, not memories, cause her to keep silent; yet through her actions, she tells her story, the truth she cannot hide. The truth surfaces in all of her small acts, refusing to be buried. Even until her death at 90, she had yet to utter a complete sentence to me, her youngest daughter, about the horror that beset her as a teen. I realized how naïve I had been in trying to help her embrace her burden. Through my mother's silence and shame, she guided me to change that which I could: myself.

Blood & Honey *demands change simply by sharing the truth. As you read the* first-person stories of war and war crimes survivors, you will be immersed in the truth and, thus, marked by it forever. Their stories will change you. Confidentiality for most of the stories is maintained by various elements that do not interrupt the bones of each account. Names are used only when permission was given.

My appeal is that you will enter the community of truth-tellers and live as though the world really is the place it should be, that you will heal and that you will take on the practices that can and do stop violence. By reading this book and sharing the truth of its people, you will be thrust into the flow of life, the present moment, and you will walk away changed, bearing the iconic tattoo of the unspoken truth.

Danica

Erin Hilleary
Artwork in based on archeological artifacts of Old Europe Vinca Period

CHAPTER 1

Definitions

Words are one of the most powerful tools we use to love, hurt, hate, and heal. My experiences have brought forth new meanings to words, and even novel vocabulary altogether, which express the feminine wisdom with which I have come to respect and understand. My understanding of women's traumas is captured by these novel concepts. I endeavor to give words back to women, to give them a voice that reflects feminine wisdom. Words cut. Unspoken words wound. But words also heal.

I am bravely sharing an ancient secret of transgenerational stories that the Western world has demanded to remain unknown. As we dip this ancient rippling circle, the *kolo* of connections, I offer an experiential read filled with storied instructions.

BALKAN- BLOOD & HONEY

In translating the word 'Balkans' we will envisage how the world is interconnected with oral memory traditions. Blood and honey are the metaphors and movements integrating into language our way of life and culture. We can view this with the literal translation for Balkans as meaning 'Blood and Honey.'

Blood and honey describes an intimate narrative, if not emotions and feelings, affecting lives of those that are not alive today but their memories are symbolically preserved in the term Balkan. Migratory patterns from the east took place thousands of years earlier moving their way into Eastern Europe, the Balkans. Those migrants entered into the land of blood and honey.

Linguistics of the word "Balkan" in Turkish is *mountain* or *rock* and the peninsula landform. However, the Iranian origin of the word "Balkan" points to the Proto-Indo European 'balagan" meaning 'something wooden." Perhaps, a folk etymology, references occur for the Turkish words 'bal' to mean honey and 'kan' for blood. Either way, what the linguistics show is the migratory patterns.

The difference between migratory patterns and diaspora is easily understood with migrations occurring for abundance not fleeing from violence. But with the Balkan War 1991-94, WWI, and WWII, we see how the term Blood and Honey now has a meaning for a century of brutal wars and diaspora.

The term blood and honey describes diverse life experiences and the ability to transform trauma events through intensified learning applications into wisdom.

BEARING WITNESS

Is the most difficult response and act I have ever done. The Bosnian women who are marginalized and erased often wondered why someone would return without the salves to soften their wounds. With little or no funding, and their invisible status to the helping aid organizations, bearing witness ties your hands behind your back as you brave the elements.

Understanding bearing witness is meant to assume the posture of trees rooted to one spot all their lives. When the trees fall to the Earth, a decaying mass transmigration into the new saplings occurs. The fallen nurse log or crumbling wood adds to the soil as if there is immense relief after being in one posture for perhaps hundreds of years. The shattered and torn fallen tree returns its energy given while alive by leaving behind its flesh filled with tree rings of recorded life as a nurse log. This is the same process for memories and the oral memory traditions.

The dendrology records- the internal witness- the environment the tree experiences. Our bodies hold memory, just like tree rings. It is the memories that shape our DNA and lives. Layering each memory, rings of experiences, we evolve and heal.

The important spiral of mourning is blocked for the Bosnian women today with the loss of bearing witness. Within the context of the interviews and my time with these women, their narratives often had their story in its entirety for the first time in their lives. The preservation of the witness enables their past experiences to be held in story and heard with the utterly crucial observed body language to a community who listens to them.

Bearing witness is an agency, enactivism where the nature of the cultural meaning is dynamically enacted.

But, the gossip, finger pointing, and blame and shame done by South Slavic women is a heightened form of horizontal violence; hubris from patriarchal indoctrination and worshipping that many Slavic women fear while being together. But, the catastrophic traumas incurred seek bearing witness which cannot be achieved while facing such female-to-female violence or the rampant male violence.

Horizontal violence destroys the nature of cultural meaning. Manmade violence and wars kill her, kill nature thus all of life.

I found out why horizontal violence was so devastating. The 'why' is found in the definition of bearing witness. Known more so among women as the space and place of "feminine being," and "female solidarity." Its' the life experiences and observation triggering transmigrations of their deep cellular memory recall. Bearing witness ennobles the victims with harmony and peaceful dimensions.

Horizontal violence doesn't transfigure into ennobling or harmony.

The resistance to the verdict perpetrated by horizontal violence took me and the Bosnian women to a knowing that survival managed to have them alive despite the violence. But, how? In having their stories in entirety, a real creative act brought to life their internal witness. Its' not the 'why' but the 'how' that evolves us.

Because isn't the horizontal violence of women's inhumanity towards women a

Through their kolos, round folk dances and circles of South Slavic women working in the fields, on their weaving, kilms or fine needle work, we are met with immediate knowing and become interactive with the unknown by bearing witness.

For those practicing the kolo, a natural haven for bearing witness, the trauma and sorrows have become integral in the mourning process akin to shifting through the ashes of their first-person stories to bank an ember and eventually a fire.

BIOCULINARY

Bioculinary arts signify agricultural and bioculinary evolution by female hands and wisdom. Bioculinary is about sustainability where food needs for present generation is met without compromising food needs for the future generations. As a social responsibility, the mother breastfeeds her child, the blood and honey term is noted, and this act is mirrored in the agriculture, gardens and herbs later in life for her family.

Organic foods that are not genetically modified, no pesticides, artificial fertilizer to sewage sledge, the Slavic women grew their gardens, maintained husbandry are a part of bio food and bioculinary efforts that heal the body. Although, bioculinary practices were done since Neolithic if not earlier, the South Slavic mothers had no choice but to grow their food needs due to a century of wars.

BIOSEMIOTICS- SOMATIC PSYCHOLOGY

Somatic psychology incorporates the body biology, and the biosemiotic includes the whole. Both focus on the signs and script not reducible to words. What is not reducible to words can be found in movements of the body and mind that heal and expresses what needs to be acknowledged and read. Often words cannot contain nor communicate these biological expressions. A good example is a passage in a book describing the smell of the roses. The words do not emit a rose scent but we know the rose scent.

It is important to note the difference between emotions and feelings for this book. Emotions are affective states. Consider the 'e' in emotions for energy or a jet fuel since emotions are moods such as depression, frustrations, irritation, and boredom to rage. Feeling states are love, joy, horror, peace, harmony to sadness. Emotions are the outer layers of the onion. Peeling back the layers through the tears and fears we reach the core, the felt states.

Bio means life and semiotic is about signs. The science of biosemiotics centers on the diverse multi-layered communications that exists in every living organisms. The affective (emotions and feelings) neuroscience field has their focus on semiotics pertaining to how the brain operates and communicates biologically. Most trauma

result of trauma and violence against her female sex?

experts know that trauma is psycho-biological but have yet, to consider biosemiotics in their fields. This is due to the sciences reductive methodologies that tear apart the whole and look at one part of the whole without understanding the inter-relationships threaded throughout.

Somatic psychology practices involve neuroscience to dance movements. Soma means living body and its' movements and energies. Oral memory traditions capture these movements passing down rituals and practices to future generations. The oral memory traditions are a supporting infrastructure housing embedded somatic psychological and physical movements to incorporate the whole body, mind, thus creating culture.

The Bosnian women's use of oral memory traditions of the *kolo-folk round dance or to be in a circle* protected them in some way. Its' roots is in the biology. Field notes support the premise of the *kolo* activity as their only supporting infrastructure since the war crimes victims and witnesses reported their invisibility in the eyes of aid organizations and the Stabilization Force (SFOR) policies.

"We had nothing. I shared a spoon with eight of us for what food we had. The *kolo* organized us seamlessly," reported the female leader of the *kolo*, a member of the witnesses group. The healing of trauma took place within the social formation of the *kolo* oral memory traditions. Biology is expressed through the kolo and social collectives.

For purposes of this book, biosemiotics takes in the whole and searches for meaning. It's about how the whole body/mind/soul is impacted by war crimes and war that has a vocabulary without words. By not just being immersed in clinical psychology with a somatics (living body) concentration, we can unravel the damage imparted by wars and rebuild into an infinitely more varied and, of course, complex healing process.

CULTURE

Culture is rooted in biology- the mother. I learned to discern between culture and the cult of violence our world is immersed in. While media, scientific studies, and political agendas lay claim to the word culture, I had to repeatedly ask the Bosnian women war crimes and war survivors "What is culture?" and "What is violence?"

When, the Bosnian grandmother would point out how her neighbor's wife did not clean well enough for her husband or put food on the table when he demanded, beating her repeatedly, I was told this was the Bosnian culture. I stood my ground and said that is violence not culture and certainly not Bosnian culture.

My kolo trauma treatment and training is a non-linear process of transformative support and responsiveness to impel social movement toward a violence-free world for women. Not just in Bosnia with the women war crimes and war survivors, I saw how the kolo either through a circle or dancing healed by surfacing the social collective process in women. The social collective is the heart of culture since it always remembers the children and does not exclude the men.

The old traditions demand rituals cycling cultures of memories. But, clearly the ruptures of the past to the present from the Balkan War and the aftermath of war thwart any reclaiming of ages of old traditions. Terms for the old ways are labeled as peasants, those not educated, and from the country. However, the old ways are a native intelligence aligned with the biology of life. The world is flesh.

Culture is not the war crimes, the domestic violence or the rape camps targeting old to young women during the Balkan war. In fact, many Bosnian women spoke of having no life during the Balkan War and in its aftermath.

What this means is without the oral memory traditions filtering in harmony and healing inducing constant change, movements, reconstruction of memories, life is not lived. And South Slavs know life is to be lived and, if not lived, there is no life.

EPIGENETICS

My insight of epigenetic inheritance is what I do daily or how I have lived life. Every movement repeated to how I live my life is passed down through the ages. I thought of a century of wars for the South Slavs, which had my great grandmother, grandmother, and mother surviving catastrophic violence and wars.

Then, came my shock after researching epigenetics and trauma.

What I learned about trauma impacts fits into one word; *transgenerational.* Just as epigenetic is transgenerational and oral memory traditions, a science of rituals that is rooted in the epigenetic processes, trauma is passed down through our DNA.

My own family maternal and paternal lineage is evidence of epigenetic inheritance gone violent away from the mother's true oral memory traditions of nurture and nature. Oral memory traditions, an epigenetic process, equips us with survival skills for Mother Nature disasters not man-made wars and violence.

It's all down to what our ancestors and your mothers to grandmothers lived that can add to the gene expressions. Since the kolo is Mesolithic in age, the same dance steps are played out today in the kolo dancing. However, the kolo dance steps are layered with new memories, perhaps, an element to the dance is added that will be passed to future generations. The same process can occur for passing down genetic diseases and programming such as Rhett syndrome- severe autism.

How this is done is with the epigenetic modifications. Researchers have cited how the cell's fate is controlled via epigenetics.[1] Epigenetic modifications cannot alter the gene codes. Instead, epigenetic modification can change *how it is expressed or not expressed.* This is rather simple definition of a very complex process.

Epi is Greek for 'at, to, over and besides. Genetics, also Greek origins – genetikos- pertains to 'origins.'

HERSTORIES ARE FIRST PERSON STORY

This is the first expression of someone's story as told by the person who experienced it. The story straight from the

1 Carey, Nessa (2012) *The Epigenetics Revolution.*

mouths of the survivors—not the condensed New York Times column. A first person story is a witnessed legend unfolding before curious ears that are willing to bear the weight of deep pain, heightened happiness, or the severely mundane. A first person story can only be collected by someone deeply curious and open to knowing as opposed to understanding. To know is to place yourself compassionately in the speaker's story, getting inside her memory to witness the pain she holds and help bear the weight of it.

First person stories can also be "told" in the sharing of images. An iconic face that speaks beyond the limits of written pages is the image of abbreviated tattooed numbers on the forearms of holocaust survivors—a perfect example of voiced story spoken by an image.

Herstories are raw, disembodied whisperings of the female holocaust filled with symbols and icons that define trauma. Trauma for a woman is the wounding that cannot be forgotten, indelibly written upon her DNA and the DNA of her children. The field of psychology recognizes Herstory as a mode of representing and sharing intergenerational trauma and its consequences, such as Post Traumatic Stress Disorder.

To blame and shame the victim foregoes any possible healing or acceptance. It also causes a lack of collaborative effort by both genders to end the intergenerational cycle of violence. Truly tragic is our ignorance and refusal of Herstories, the raw life experiences that could save the world from repeating its crimes against humanity. As it is, the media and its patriarchal words normalize crimes against females and humanity in a world of violence. Calling the perpetrators of violence "victors" merely lionizes them and further establishes their actions as dominant; this semantic shift is how the media has turned itself into a soap opera, existing to generate revenue though "hooking" viewers. I feel a chill whenever the term "collateral damage" is bandied about by the representatives of the military and other male-dominated institutions.

The final insult of trauma wounds is that no one asks the victim for her first person story. What is often worse than the trauma event itself is being chastised for indiscriminately pouring her heart to all who pass by her in life. She is labeled as talking too much or talking nonsense, while history celebrates his traumatic event as heroic, his suffering god-like. I need to accept that each one of us—myself included—has passed by these victims both knowingly and unknowingly in our rush to maintain denial and increase the speed of avoidance.

I think of the hundreds and thousands of women who have died and never been worthy of someone asking about their lives. Pore through the annals of history or the media for the past two thousand years, and you see that the pens writing the words are in the hands of men. These written records reflect entropy, showing us the deterioration of feminine worth for generations. This is never said or written upon the pages of memory. The problem of the silent woman is a giant tidal wave, wiping away oral tradition. It becomes a hard and fast rule, a truly abnormal state to entrap females, especially the mothers of sons. The rule is to inquire only to be titillated or to reveal the perverse, but a woman's first person story is not entertainment. For me, it is searing to hear the only words spoken about my mother's concentration camp experience from a male, my maternal great-uncle. Equally burning and caustic was the single sentence from my father about the smell from the concentration camp chimneys in a paper for my master's degree program.

As I noted with my parents and most who survived war and violence, instead of sealing wounds with earnest witness-bearing, they seal their voices in mute shame. Males are especially shamed to be placed in the "female" victim position. I witnessed my parents' survivorship of WWII and refugee status perpetuating his male insecurity, which then pervaded the home, funneling into domestic violence as his male cultural entitlement.

HERSTORY

Herstory is the untold experiences of those who have been excluded from history. Rather than a play-by-play of events and facts, a person's herstory is told in all forms, from dance to poetry, rituals to tears. These are the experiences that fulfill the listener's passionate questioning, the answers that cannot be revealed by traditional interrogation. Herstory becomes forgotten in the search for records and facts, leaving this experiential truth to stay locked away in the deepest, yet often simplest, of cultural rituals. Herstory includes silent words that are spoken between the lines, the words we miss when all we do is hear. Unlike history, herstory often goes unwritten, unbound by male logic.

The secret behind herstory is its ability to elucidate a procession of first-person stories, though not simply from spoken words or texts, but from relationships and icons. In the form of dance, herstory combines experiences with movement, each beat of music signifying an action or emotion. In this way, the South Slavic tradition of dancing the kolo, the round dance performed in many forms across different contexts, is actually a physical manifestation of herstory. *Her words can dance.* Her words can have a structure tuned to the verses of song. The kolo is a metaphor for how women must stand shoulder-to-shoulder in order to chant their stories to the world. These circular processions of first-person stories define the *storied instructions* you will see in the following chapters.

The term gynikomenemonikothanasia[2] describes the pervasive male bias in society that has resulted in the exclusion or belittlement of all feminine aspects of history. There are no tender inquiries from us that simmer into delicious and fragrant rituals. This leaves nothing that speaks of women, the female voice, to add to our sound-bite-driven world of media as fact. There is no arrangement of vocabulary that speaks clearly and truthfully about violence against women, yet fits neatly into a 140-character Twitter update.

It is fruitless to insert the secret herstories of women into the vast collection of male history. Too often, they are viewed as attacks from women, who are then defensively labeled as man-haters. Herstories become a global swamp of defensive and offensive reactions to the prevailing masculine society. There has been no tender cradling of women's herstory, as we have not yet learned to ask women to truly share their traumatic stories.

2 Davis, E. G. (1971). *The first sex.* New York: G.P. Putnam's Sons.

This book goes beyond the spoken and written word contained in the six letters of *trauma*, surpassing the histories written in masculine-focused pages. It is difficult to capture onto pages of text the metaphoric movement of herstory, such as the swaying rhythm of the kolo dances. But silence results in the vilification of women, so this book attempts to portray the stories as unambiguously as possible, leaving the gruesome, yet healing, mental images, raw emotions, and ultimate peace to transcend the written text. The sincerity of sharing and asking others to share their intimate lives brings forth a state of grace that descends as if from an ancient Slavic goddess. It is in Her collective wisdom that we have the ability to heal.

HERSTORY TRAUMA

Herstory Trauma healing by the women is clear and consistent by developing new realities to construct history along with herstory as their future and to have the past acknowledging their narratives and existence. Through artful ethnochoreology, herstories record their efforts facing weakness, vulnerabilities, and hostilities with compassion for themselves.

The past is viewed from a female narrative, specifically a feminist perspective and issues that are omitted in history. Origins of herstory are from the late 1960's with the great Women's Liberation movement and from a thorough review of conventional history. However, the word history comes from ancient Greek meaning "knowledge by inquiry".

Let me list the ever escalating civilian causalities in global conflicts and wars: trafficking of women 98% of estimated 4.5 million forced into sexual exploitation and; women in urban developing countries are twice as likely to experience violence; all the women killed in 2012 close to 505 were killed by intimate partners or family members. Women's herstories are facing an apocalypse.[3]

KOLO

The word is quite old, perhaps stretching back into Sanskrit, but is known within Indo- European origins meaning the wheel. Old Church Slavonic kolo and Russian 'koleso' (wheel) is the kolo which means to dance or to be in a circle. The Kolo is movement.

Our biology, our cells are replenishing our bodies on a cyclical process, basically, a biological dance and constant movements. What is microscopic is but the macro for our bodies and life world. The repeating steps of the Slavic kolo dances such as U Sest (six) step is but our biological processes right down to our DNA which replicates.

The term Slavic Moist Mother Earth is a metaphor if not an algorithm for 366 degree circle. Often Slavic mythology contains language of the earth being round, pregnant and gestation. The seasons are celebrated with rituals and dances commemorating the kolo dance our planet does in the cosmos.

3 United Nations Facts & Figures: Ending violence against Women, a pandemic in diverse forms http://www.unwomen.org/en/what-we-do/ending-violence-against-women/facts-and-figures

The *kolo* practices are rooted in making sense of traumatic effects and replacing traumatic memories with healing life experiences, all via the roles of mothers and daughters. Since the female body is homologic (biology shared across ancestry, having a common origin), the circle of the *kolo* represents further unification of the women's bodily heritage as they move in synchrony in the same place and space.

But, the oral memory traditions with practices such as the kolo observed in the Bosnian women war crimes and war survivors are riddled with effects of war and genocide. The kolo, became the meeting space and place, either in the dance or the circle and was carried through to the aftermath of war.

Survivorship of war crimes, the intermediate functioning of the potential space, occurs via the body, corporeality, language, images, and shared symbols. The Bosnian women war crimes and war survivors had continuous exposure to one another in the aftermath, rather than during the war, in which many were refugees who were fleeing from violence.

An aspect of the *kolo* indicates a healing ritual via the embodiment of female roles during traumatic events. By taking the fleeing movement of refugees into the kolo dances, the movement is given space and place to organize memory within a social collective.

The kolo produces a social collective in harmony with each other, and the world we live in. Science is just barely catching up to what our ancestors already understood and lived. For instance, recent findings show community as healing agent, if not, a cure for addictions.

ORAL MEMORY TRADITIONS

We know before the alphabet and words on the page, pre-literate cultures used repetition of body, food to stories to pass down storied instructions into memory. The survival memories ensured the species life across generations which are etched into our DNA and epigenetic processes. For instance, we know that babies have an inherited fear of snakes.

Oral memory traditions is memory preserved and perpetuated into community and community into culture. Like culture, oral memory traditions are rooted in our biology.

But, what is so resilient and resourceful within the South Slavic oral memory traditions that is easily perpetuated throughout the generations despite the numerous wars, conquests, or other formidable obstacles?

It presents as another narrative to involve an intensified learning application that if added to modern era academia, education programs and training breeds an extraordinarily different global perspective of conceiving the world as indivisible.

Especially, significant, the South Slavs managed without a written alphabet until the late 1800's. One result of having a late start on the Latin alphabet, the Serbo-Croatian language has the status of being the most perfect written language in the world according to many linguists. In a spatial fashion of having the perfect written language, translating the South Slavic language provides a startling insight to millennium aged words and terms that has not been doctored with our modern era twenty-six lettered alphabet.

Oral and written language is a dimension of oral memory traditions that preserves permanence of life well lived or meaningful. The oral memory practice is to cherish through the rituals and practical daily life. We need to remember the mother manifests language and culture. The mother is the biological roots of culture.

Oral memory traditions conveyed for thousands of years rituals, commemorative ceremonies, and birth and death performativity, domestic organizational processes to include husbandry and agriculture. Either through song, folk dances such as the round dance called Kolo for South Slavs, textiles to embroidery, any and all movement of the body as it revolved in their life world was illuminated so as to have the memory applied in present day. The importance of passing down the life experiences of ancestors is a learning intensive classroom. In a sense, what you learned at your mother's knee or at your father's side at a craft meant life lived meaningfully preserved in the oral memory traditions.

POETIC COLLEGE

The poetic college is a space of storied instructions. The poetic college sees the instructions in a story without a professor to point out the rules. The poetic college chooses to take a lesson from a simple story instead of allowing that story to fade into oblivion as pure entertainment or a passing moment. The poetic college learns from what has passed in an active, intensified way that validates the storyteller as a teacher of pain, joy, happiness, or sadness.

The curricula of storied instructions flourish within a poetic college. Enrollment into the poetic college is often induced by traumatic events. What I discovered is that trauma in the Paleolithic and Neolithic age is the origin of the need for a poetic college. The poetic college is a learning environment that instructs us in thriving, not surviving. Whatever rippled and connected to the ancient Neolithic or Paleolithic past demanded that secret Herstories be revealed to nourish their audience.

Survival skills were once an intensified learning, a true poetic college. People gathered resiliency skills over the years from natural disasters and cataclysmic events, and they passed these skills down through the generations. This has now translated into the repeating of victim behaviors instead of the proactive ability to adapt as we follow the patterns of those who came before us, normalized through written history and proliferated throughout culture. There is no choice in being a victim, since it is pressed upon the flesh and blood throughout the generations, but nonetheless, those with the iconic numbers tattooed on their bodies face being called victims, as if this makes them weak, not just people to whom something traumatic has happened. They are ripe for further judgment, pity, and blame, as others wonder why they allowed such things to happen. As the blame and shame cloaks the victims, the offenders gain distance from any consequences; they are simply patriots or pillars of justice in the new linguistic that they devise to describe the aftermath of violence. I hear this in myself when I have stated in the past that I would rather work with men than women or when women who misunderstand the term posit that they are not feminists since they do not hate men. If we women truly loved men and our sons, would our silence that nods assent to masculine violence ever exist?

PSYCHOLOGICAL GAP

The psychological gap, in this context, is the abyss between a mother's love for her children of both sexes and her subtle privileging of her male children-sons. This gap explains why we support our sons as they return from war, but we fail to advocate for our daughters who have been by other mothers' sons in the same war. This psychological gap allows us to support our husbands, brothers, and sons as they fight and kill other men, all the while denying to ourselves that these men are other women's husbands, brothers, and sons. The gap is an abyss of denial that both connects and divides our shared humanity.

To this day, in the former Yugoslavia, a mother's worth is based on the number of sons she has birthed. It is widely believed among South Slavic peoples that a son loves his mother in the same ancestral fashion as his Neolithic ancestors loved and revered the Moist Mother Earth above all others. However, there remains an often overlooked discrepancy between mothers' offspring; by measuring a son's love of his mother and her actual worth by the number of sons she has birthed, her daughters are left to face gender violence in catastrophic proportions. If patriotism's lethal impact remains unchecked for its neglect of narratives that proclaim herstory, we will inevitably witness the horrors of the past five thousand years again.

For example, with my mother being a WWII concentration camp survivor, am I begging the readers to say it isn't true that my mother was said to have strangled infants and thrown the little bodies into the furnace just to keep her own family fed? Since it was my Maternal Great Uncle who told me what my mother did in the Jasenovac, am I preferring the avoidance, the denial that most men and women perform every moment of their lives to go on with this so-called life? No. My mother's and other women's narratives are dangerous; many want them left unsaid, kept hidden from the patriarchal rule of law and its courts. I am begging readers to stop the violence of silence; I am begging female readers to speak for women and, in doing so, to include our sons. Because isn't the horizontal violence of women's inhumanity towards women a result of trauma and violence against her female sex?

Hidden in gossip and so-called idle speech, violence towards women rears its head in finger-pointing, blame, and shaming of our sisters. The silence blinds us and continually gives freedom to men to commit reoccurring violence in ignorance of its true impact, especially on the women who surround them. The silence of a female community that watches multiple men rape the town outcast in the square, a practice that has occurred over generations, or witness through the millennia the constant slaughter of the feminine nature is what we need to evolve beyond. The immense social, psychological, and somatic practices within female humanities and the female capacity to forge culture have evolved our species—or perhaps have allowed it to devolve. We once knew female solidarity that engendered and prompted peaceful societies. Can we recapture that?

What equally contributes to and perpetuates the constant slaughter of feminine nature is best stated by Mary Condren of the Institute for Feminism and Religion in Ireland: "If I were to cite the single greatest obstacle for a woman today it would be the internalized oppression, the oppression derived from women who have not become conscious of their status as colonized people and who are still arguing and squabbling, scrambling over the mountains of snow set up by the patriarchy. Her death has come, not at the hands of men, but at the hands of women oblivious of the system that enslaves them all."[4]

For years, I have observed other conditions of complete ignorance found existing in a state of side-by-side silence. The psychological gap allows South Slavic mothers to prize their sons over their daughters without realizing what they are doing or the impact that this privileging will have on their daughters and granddaughters. For most of my professional life in trauma, I look at the patriotism that prompts mothers to send their sons off to war, ostensibly to protect those left behind. The patriarchy reinforces the idea that a woman is worth the number of sons she provides, which both obliterates her femininity and produces more men for those in power to use in subduing others, both their own female family and the citizens of both genders in an "enemy" nation.

When I endeavor to discover from the mothers of soldiers more information about the participation of their sons in the militaries of Africa, Bosnia, or Sri Lanka, I face the psychological gap that presents in the face of male-on male-violence justified and perpetuated by mothers. My question confronts the mothers, wives, daughters, and sisters whose male relatives marched off to war to protect them. The question: "Was it your husband, father, uncle, brother, or son who killed her father, uncle, brother, or son over there?" And I pose this question to those of us from privileged countries: How do we label those people "over there?"

STORIED INSTRUCTIONS

Storied instructions are fed by memory; oral memory practices. Memory is biological and embodied working with our wondrous neurological system, our brains, and the soma, our living bodies. Essentially, storied instructions are a technology to purposely retrieve full access to our knowing.

Knowing is not knowledge that requires tomes, physical libraries, academic, and training institutions. Knowing moves past the need to break it down to understand and goes to the heart with complete wisdom, compassion, and growth.

Shaping our DNA is our life experiences and the environment. Both life experiences and our environment, the nature and nurture storied instructions I learned from the Bosnian women concerns their capacity to soak in and to record in memory held in their bodies the truths given and exposed.

Shifting to a social collective, the communal is a vast array through storied instruction. The broader implications of storied instructions

4 ED. Joan Marler, *From the Realm of the Ancestors, Anthology in Honor of Marija Gimbutas,* (Knowledge, Ideas & Trends, Inc., 1997) p. 422

enters into a realm of the social collective, a communal mind that is immersed in infinite awareness, whole and complete. In other words, we are born with all the storied instructions and knowing.

I had often received but appreciated the shock and my sense of violation that rose up in full force of female rage when hearing the insufferable, the misery, and the violence. But, storied instructions will instigate an abandonment of our infatuation with individuality channeling rage into the creative bearing witness.

Instead, with storied instructions I am faced with letting go the concept of the standalone ruggedly independent individual. I find myself moving into a pathway igniting the capacity to bear witness. Storied instructions are not about judging or analysis rather, it's not about right or wrong or opinions which are just a single point of view not all of the views. Storied instructions is not about getting to understanding but it is about accepting all as it is. But, accepting all it is will not have victim-hood or martyrdom.

Storied instructions are inescapable. The social collective is communal offering unanticipated insights and awareness that cannot be smothered by smart phones, ipads, or iphones. Storied instructions provide a critical and integral experience of knowing extrapolating reason that I had not ever previously understood before because it is not about understanding. Its' about knowing.

Instead of having the intellectual knowledge that we are all connected with one another, I *know* we are all related.

TRAUMA

Trauma is psycho-biological. The flight/fright we have when facing dire situations has the hormones flooding the body before we are even conscious of it. This is communications without words.

In fact, we have an autonomic (operates without consciousness) process. Breathing is autonomic, but when we focus on breathing such as in yoga or dancing, we can consciously change our breathing rhythm. Most do not know that the simple cure for trauma impacts is to breathe and more importantly, the exhale. The exhale is the only exit for adrenalin to leave our bodies.

Trauma yields no language to what happened to you since such an event never did happen before. What I learned from the Bosnian women was to get comfortable with the uncomfortable passage through answerlessness where we are silenced and mute before such raw power. It is when we move through what happened and its aftermath that we speak and orient to the meaning of what happened.

I learned trauma is a biological exploration of memory processes and experiences we encounter in life. Not at all pathological, trauma and memories resulted in our survival. But, there is a point where we need to ask do we need to survive or thrive. I found by switching from survival to thriving takes three elements; intense curiosity, awe and to still wonder about life. With any of these three elements, the internal witness or the person bearing witness needs to be present.

The biosemiotics in trauma is communicated in the symbolic memory with its repeated possession by the traumatized person. Intrusive dreams, hallucinations, dreams, thoughts or behaviors stemming from the trauma experience can have numbing and avoidance. Note the lack of words but the rich communications and how the trauma takes over the victim.

Trauma impacts often fail to connect to feelings and experiences. Trauma has a structure that is very difficult for victims to verbalize and if the victim manages, the trauma is poorly verbalized. And it is for a very good reason; to block the pain and distress. However, what I observed with the Bosnian women through their oral memory traditions and daily life would connect the emotions (affects, moods such as anxiety, depression, frustration, anger, etc.) as biosemiotic signals to heal.

Trauma for me is intensified learning even though the traumatic event is difficult and catastrophic. Trauma is not an illness. Nor are the biosemiotic signals to heal. According to Dabrowski, the science of positivism he states "without passing through very difficult experiences and even something like psychoneurosis and neurosis we cannot understand human beings and we cannot realize our multidimensional and multilevel development toward higher and higher levels."

Connie Simpson

CHAPTER 2

Storied Aprons

A VISIT TO AHMICA-VITTEZ, BOSNIA

Just days after September 11, 2001, I had scheduled a trip back to Bosnia to continue trauma treatment and training with Bosnian women who were survivors of war and war crimes. I received a voicemail from my son, warning me of the great danger I would face in Bosnia in the 9-11 aftermath. My husband, equally nervous, demanded that I not go. Only my daughter encouraged me to travel. I rarely make decisions based on fear, so I boarded the plan from Seattle to New York.

The plane only stopped in New York to catch a direct flight to Amsterdam. I had never been to New York for any other reason than flight connections. This layover was quite different though, with extraordinarily long security lines and enforcement of security in this American airport as tight as those in Europe. During the long wait, I watched as security officers pulled random people out of line for individual checks. Most of those who were singled out were Muslim or of Arab descent. I noticed myself sweating as I stood in the long lines, and I recognized this as a symptom of the indirect trauma I was experiencing.

During the long wait, I thought of the Bosnian mother who spoke to me about the searches and violent demands for papers and identity cards during the Balkan War. The Croat and Serb militaries and armed insurgents used these searches throughout the former Yugoslavia to identify civilians who had Muslim first names. This mother's son had been summarily shot during a seemingly innocuous search in the middle of Novi Travnik, simply because the enemy had read his first name. His body was left in the middle of town for days.

While waiting, I glanced out of the broad glass windows and searched the skyline of New York for its notable twin towers. The realization of their absence forced tears from my eyes as I thought of the innocent civilians who had suffered horrific deaths right here, on our own U.S. soil. I thought of the thousands of mothers whose sons and daughters had died that day. Six years later at the Women's Peace Conference in Dallas, I came face-to-face with the widow of a man who had been murdered in the 9-11 attack. The woman's husband had been killed because he was an American who had worked circumstantially at the terrorists' target, the Twin Towers. The widow's trauma was manifested in her tears, as well as in my hands that shook after hearing about her tragic loss. It was then that I realized it does not matter whether we are Muslims, Arabs, or Americans; we are all next in line. We are all targets of some enemy.

I was welcomed with open arms at the end of my journey when I arrived in Novi Travnik to meet the group of Bosnian women who made up the Sumejja Kolo. They were elated to greet me on their doorstep so soon after 9-11. The women had feared reprisals and my withdrawal from them because of their Muslim status. I told them that we are all daughters before any other status or citizenship. All of the women expressed heartfelt pain for the horror that was too familiar to them; their empathy with America was strong, especially with the families who had lost loved ones in the tragic attacks. I later wrote the following section about Storied Aprons on my return home from Bosnia. I remember searching my kitchen once I was home and discovering that I did not have an apron in which to place my tissues or shaking hands.

Ahmica-Vitez War Crimes site Kolo Sumejja women visit

STORIED APRONS

The Croatian enclave in the village of Ahmica is literally separated by a two-lane highway from the Muslim enclave. You can have a pleasant conversation across the narrow highway if no cars are screaming by. On the Croatian side, a Catholic church stands squarely facing the road. Against the backdrop of crops and cows, it creates an imposing figure on the otherwise pastoral landscape. The ruined, desecrated mosque lies in scattered heaps on the Muslim side. You would think you could see this twisted, concrete and steel structure from the highway, but you cannot. The brief glimpses we had of the mosque ruins as we walked through the small streets were both traumatizing and heart-wrenching. It seemed to flicker in our peripheral vision and then disappear again. In the end, the ruined mosque competed with the very visible upright posture of the Croatian church.

First-time visitors gasp when they arrive at the mosque and witness the immensity of the hatred that wreaked such destruction on this holy structure, making a flimsy wreck of the once-strong steel and stone. The minaret lay on its side, emblazoned with scrawled graffiti, "F*** your Turkish mother." Upon viewing the mess during my visit in 2006, my reaction was to clasp my hands over my ears as if to drown out the cacophony, though there was not a sound in the air.

As fate would have it, the anniversary of the Ahmica war crimes massacre in 2006 fell on Easter Sunday. Tension hung in the air, erecting an invisible barrier that emanated across the two-lane highway. That day, the mourning of the Ahmica memorial unintentionally competed with the Croatians as they erected their

huge, neon cross. These ghoulishly synchronized dates perpetuated the trauma of the war survivors, many of whom watched the men the killers of their families as they erected the massive unmistakable icon of their differences. Somehow, the neon cross did not harmonize with the Catholic church's beautiful architecture, nor with the elderly Croatian grandmother who I watched as she stood in the church yard providing a bit of beauty and peace to counteract the blazing sign of defiance.

As I approached the Croatian grandmother to request permission to take her photograph, she smiled at me. She twisted her apron in her hands and was about to answer me when a stout, aggressive man interrupted. "Who are you?" he demanded. I responded that my name was Danica Anderson. He smiled when he heard my name, stating that it was a good old Yugoslav first name but that the only thing wrong was my last name. I shrugged and told him that I had married an American. I did not dare tell him that my parents were Serbs, nor did I mention my work with the Muslim women. I asked his permission to take a photo, and he grandly gestured his permission. I glanced over to the elderly grandmother and noticed her still twisting a corner of her apron.

Names hold great importance among Bosnians, as evidenced by both the man's sharp recognition of my name and the unbridled massacres of those with Muslim names in prior years. The villages and towns in the former Yugoslavia are named for the many families who inhabit them. For example, in the town of Ahmica, most residents share the last name *Ahmica* or could at least trace their direct ancestry back to that family name. So it came to be that the destruction of the town was considered to be the destruction of the family as well.

The Muslim Ahmica grandmothers who had survived the war crimes massacre on April 16th, 1993, had once shared their tragic story with me. The women were in the field with the cows during the early morning hour, their waists cloaked in aprons that were often stained with a patina of blazing copper. The women's efforts at pristine laundering by scrubbing with their wide South Slavic hands were fruitless. I often heard that copper coloring on the apron was worn as a flag, having been stained by the raw earth, the blood of birthing babies, or the slaughter of livestock. That day, however, the women's aprons were soaked with blood and tears from the slaughter of their own families.

The turmoil of WWI and WWII had revisited their families with hatred, not from some enemy across distant borders, but from neighbors and friends who shared their fence lines and land. The women had used their aprons to comfort each other's screams, wiping away tears of shock, trauma, and disbelief, as horror burst from them. The incredibly vulnerable

"I think of other grandmothers having such a loss, and I cannot hate what I am," she stated.

and graceful elderly women and grandmothers came to know the hatred of mass murder that occurs from neighbor to neighbor, friend to friend, and woman to woman.

As I met with the grandmothers over the years, I noticed a pattern they repeated often during our gatherings. The women's worn aprons were used to wipe teary eyes and to clean dirty hands from labor; this universal gesture among them symbolized their trauma and hatred, but also their comforting and healing. During my visits to Bosnia, I would often sit next to one Ahmica grandmother who had barely spoken since the slaughter of her family on April 16th. After three long years of sitting next to this woman who was cloaked in silence, she once reached over, grasped my hands in hers, and sobbed. She gathered her apron and dabbed away my tears and then hers. No words were spoken, but as I looked down at the wet but clean apron, stained with tears, I felt the love she had for her lost ones who were now in their graves. My tears soaked into the apron along with hers. I was startled to feel a lack of hatred in this woman—a complete absence of desire for retaliation or revenge after the loss of many members of her immediate family. I looked up into her face. She spoke as if she had heard my thoughts, saying, "I think of other grandmothers having such a loss, and I cannot hate what I am," she stated.

I had often wondered what each grandmother kept in her apron pockets; I eventually asked the women if I could peek into the pockets as they aprons hung on hooks in their kitchens at the end of a long day in the fields. I found the expected implements, like scissors, thread, and wire, but there were also treasures that surpassed the value of any jewel. Most of the pockets held pictures of loved ones who had died in the massacre; these photos in the old apron pockets evoked in me painful feelings of sadness and loss. Interestingly, quite a few pockets held seeds placed in scraps of paper.

I remembered the apron pockets of an old, wise grandmother I met, who we called the *stari Baba*. In her apron pockets, she kept the remnants of a doll. She would not tell me whose doll it was, but as tears plastered her wrinkled face, which had been browned by the sun, I knew the remnants triggered remembrance and mourning for her. I marveled at the *stari Baba's* intuitive mystical knowledge, visible through her map of wrinkles, and her ability to channel trauma into peace. Not a word was spoken, but we communicated through tears, hugs, and aprons.

As I continued my intrusive yet innocent search through the apron pockets, my hands shook. The aprons flagged the space and place for me to bear witness. I was robbed of my tool kit of words, my copious academic notes, media sound bites—there was no cheat sheet to help me speak meaningfully to these grief-stricken women who allowed me to meddle in their most prized possessions. I remained in the presence of my true professors, my own *stari Babas*, and begged myself to never become the professor in their midst, to never substitute the clinical for the human. Moving further into their grief,

I begged that I would never have the unfortunate opportunity to gain their particular insight, as I could not fathom losing my own loved ones and friends in order to be part of such terrible wisdom and never-ending pain.

❧ ❧

The word *remnants* come from *remains*, and the original meaning is *to stay, to put back in place*, or *to stay behind*. Associated with the words *manor*, *mansion*, and *permanent*, *remnants* provide fetal materials to birth new life when death appears. Befittingly, the youngest victim of the Ahmica war crimes was an infant whose life was aborted along with 150 of her Ahmica relatives; their lives whittled down to remnants of the past. I often pondered a compelling, nagging question: "Where do we put the remains in our lives? What do we do with the personal effects of departed loved ones?"

To help me formulate an answer to this question, I reviewed South Slavic ethnic costumes. The logic behind my inquiry into Slavic costumes was simple. South Slavic folk dancers' costumes always include an apron.

In Bulgaria with Joan Marler's[1] 2005 tour to see Slavic round dances, I was able to ask a grandmother dressed in the regional folk costume about the importance of the apron in the cultural dress. The grandmother explained in Slavic poetic words that the apron is an essential icon of female biology, which can create life and even portend destiny.

When I asked the same question to the South Slavic war and war crimes survivors, their answers evolved into the same reasoning as that of their Bulgarian Slavic sisters, essentially defining an archetypal movement or act. The apron for Slavic women is an archetype expressing female humanities and first-person stories. Much as a platonic form stands for all variants of the same object, the apron can represent any number of women, from great-grandmothers carrying crumpled photographs in their apron pockets to tiny infants whose mothers dry their tears on apron hems.

Many of the grandmothers spoke of wearing their aprons as they helped to birth a child, using the clean, familiar cloth to wipe down the infant's skin. Others spoke of burying the apron that they wore to a birth with the placenta wrapped in it under their designated sacred tree to honor the possibilities and potentials a child brings into the world. After the Balkan war, in the town of Travnik, about two kilometers from Ahmica, a mother spoke of how she cradled a man's head with her apron as he lay dying in the road. Her apron helped her provide peace to an unknown mother's son.

❧ ❧

The first-person stories that Bosnian women shared with me on this trip prompted me to face a terribly hard question: "What can I do with what I have witnessed or been told?" I had no space or place, no feminine vocabulary, to write on the pages of a book the depth and breadth of the needless, catastrophic trauma that these women had survived and, in fact, were actively surviving every day. I struggled for over ten years, if not for most of my life, to write this book of lived, not merely spoken, events.

1 Joan Marler organized the 2005 dance tour to Bulgaria in collaboration with Anna Ilieva and Anna Shturbanova, through the Institute of Archeomythology Institute, http://www.archaeomythology.org/

What I learned and observed were scrawling messages found in the most unlikely spaces and places. I had only to look for the aprons to know that the feminine vocabulary is written upon the fabric of their life experiences, woven into it. Some people might see a stained apron, but I see a tapestry of survival. I knew I had to somehow translate the story of the Ahmica grandmothers through the medium of their aprons.

I was inspired by looking at those aprons and knowing—truly *knowing*—the stories of these women. I resolved to explain to the world how to listen to women by noticing the details of their lives. The apron is the true flag and first coat of arms. Though it has been overshadowed by masculine icons like the blacksmith's apron or even the lead apron worn by a patient during an x-ray, the symbolic wisdom in a woman's apron shows us a connected life, one that spans birth and death, one that crosses generations.

What has happened to the apron and its true meaning? What if the women surviving the aggression and violence had kept their blood-soaked aprons and waved the tattered cloth as they marched as a global collective? Would this icon still remain in the shadows or would we see the wisdom pouring from it?

Connie Simpson

CHAPTER 3

Maternal Fright

WHERE AND WHEN I BORE WITNESS

Between the years 2001 through 2010, I visited Bosnia-Herzegovina to work with Ahmica women who survived war crimes in the Balkan War. In March of 2010, I arranged the annual Women's International Day conference and the Kolo trauma work tenth anniversary with speakers from around the globe and a presentation given by documentary film artist Gudrun Frank. The ten years span with the women war crimes and war survivors emphasized a vital life source through their first person stories.

INHERITANCE AND STORIED INSTRUCTIONS

The related concepts of maternal fright and intergenerational trauma are exemplified in the story of a pregnant Ahmica woman with whom I provided a trauma treatment session in 2003. A decade earlier, her husband's relatives had been massacred in Ahmica. Her name is important; however, for confidentiality purposes, I will honor her privacy and simply call her Almira. Her story remains a haunting memory of the village during the Balkan War of the 1990s.

Almira, the young and very pregnant Muslim wife, described to me how her husband's family had been decimated, as she poignantly whispered of loss and the repression of female genealogies. She spoke so softly that I had to lean forward on the worn sofa in her drab grey apartment to hear her cascade of words that would remain etched in my mind. Female genealogies are *herstories*, the inheritance of family legacy that often goes untold throughout the generations but are lived in experiences. In the case of Almira's husband's, his family had lost nearly twenty family members in one morning. The Balkan war crimes had obliterated whole family lines, relentlessly expunging family names and wiping out entire lines of female genealogies, the women whose cultural positions had been to share traditions with future generations. Almira explained that according to the International Criminal Tribunal for the Former Yugoslavia, she and her husband's family had been listed simply as *Witnesses A to Z*, in the court's attempt to maintain confidentiality, which had inadvertently disregarded the treasured family name.

As I sat there with Almira, I thought about my prior search for the meaning of trauma. I tapped my experiences with my clinical psychology doctorate and forensic psychotherapy when I had dwelled deeper into the root of trauma, knowing that I would better understand the experiences of Almira and her relatives from this perspective. Months earlier, I had become fixated on understanding the true meaning of the word *trauma*, so I had researched its origins, which were not easily found. I learned that *trauma* has Greek and Indo-European roots, but I already knew that far older words with Slavic and Old European roots speak of Mother Nature as the root of natural traumatic events, such as storms and natural disasters. In contrast, the Greek and Indo-European roots of the word refer specifically to manmade trauma, a type of trauma that seeks to outdo Mother Nature's fury. Manmade violence has become gruesome, a grotesque hijacking of the intergenerational wisdom that was meant to be passed down to thrive, not merely survive, after traumatic events.

I thought about the alternate definitions of *trauma* that meant *to wound* and *to rub or turn*, as I watched Almira's constant affectionate rubbing of her swollen belly while twinges of angst appeared in her shaking hands. The state of one's mental health creates not only substantial lasting damage to the psyche, such as in Post-Traumatic Stress Disorder (PTSD), but also manifests through physical, or psychosomatic, manifestations, such as shaking hands. Trauma, specifically, impacts the psyche as well, often leading to neurosis and to physical illness or disease. Almira's shaking hands provided me with a fuller definition of *trauma* than those found on paper.

❧ ☙

Intergenerational trauma perpetuates the effects of genocide and gynocide and the resulting trauma. Instead of learning skills that foster resiliency, today's daughters and sons learn about trauma and inherit its horrors as they effect family life. Standing before me in her living room, Almira described the murder of two generations of her grandmothers who had been killed immediately, starved, or sent to concentration camps during WWII. She asked me if the holocaustic memories of these women would be passed on from her to her unborn child. Fearing what she had heard from other elderly women, she struggled with the probability that the fetus had absorbed her grandmothers' trauma and terror through her blood and womb.

Almira would not have the opportunity to pass down her maternal grandmother's wisdom and recipes for a harmonious life that had allowed other women to thrive beyond survival. This fact left an open wound in Almira's psyche, which had been further rubbed raw by the fate of her husband's grandmother, a victim of the Ahmica massacre. I watched this young mother-to-be as she bit her thin lips, her pale skin mottled with fear, as she expressed the horror of her own memories of the Balkan War. It became clear to me that she had been worrying about whether her own memories were being transferred to her unborn child and, if so, whether the child would also absorb the violence and horror that she felt daily as she remembered her slain family.

After the UN and other humanitarian agencies created hype among the victims by saying that they would help these people, Almira expected that I would have the answers she sought, that I could tell her if her child was somehow receiving her memories through genetically-encoded violence. I knew, though, that the agencies' offers of help were fundamental efforts to expand their bureaucracy, to ensure their salaries from the European Union—not to offer fortune-telling services to those who were suffering. I braced myself to be authentic with Almira, to share honestly that I did not have a definite answer rather than hiding my inability to know for certain. I responded to her thin arms and swollen belly by saying, "I came here for you to *show me* if your memories are carried on in your child."

As I studied her small, bony fingers and wrists, Almira told me she was growing thinner from living in constant fright, while others grew fat as they sought physical comfort through eating. As we continued to drink her thick Bosnian coffee, I noticed the fading end-of-winter daylight that seeped into the room. Almira shared with me that she felt constant fear in her home, the very place where she should have felt comfort and safety as she awaited the arrival of her child. Pointing out her window, which was lined with assorted plastic buckets of dirt and compost for growing vegetables, she said that the same terror she felt spilled onto the small rural streets of Ahmica. She said that fright never left her side, even when she was in the nearby town of Novi Travnik, Bosnia. That fear, the one that invaded her home and followed her out of her village, pursued her into plans for her child's future. Her real horror, she told me, the one that made her scream in the night, was her thoughts of the rich earth that surrounded her home, which was at that time still littered with a million landmines that waited to claim more victims, perpetuating the horrors of a war that the rest of the world thought was over.

Union. Author: Erin Hilleary

Almira's husband's fright, the residual impact of losing so many family members in a single morning, would seep into her when they lied under the covers at night. His tears signified the ceaseless cry for blood-retribution, a pervasive thought among victims that contributed to the widening ethnic divide between Croats and Muslims. Almira had become so upset when she shared this with me, that she shouted a desperate question to me: "How can I bring my child into this world?"

Suddenly, Almira grabbed a green magic marker from the table, lifted her shirt over her belly, and drew a large spiral that circled around her gestating belly. She claimed that she was ensorcelling her child, magically protecting him from trauma and victimization. She believed that her spontaneous spiral ritual would prevent the horrors she had been sharing with me from crossing over to her child, to prevent them from creating in her another victim of the Balkan War. For a few precious minutes, her spell worked, and her maternal fright dissipated as the moist green magic marker scrawled the icon of a spiral. I knew now that magic is different from fantasy; Almira's South Slavic sorcery did protect her child, because her desire for peace consumed her horror, at least for a moment. Under Almira's wise tutelage, her husband and her unborn child would come to embrace the intensive learning environment that trauma brought to them as opposed to adding more fear that fed on holocaustic memories. Drawing a spiral in magic marker is a small act, one that seems meaningless, but for Almira, it represented true magic as it infused the moment with the extraordinary.

Why had Almira spontaneously chosen the shape of a spiral? I knew that she was not familiar with the writings of archaeologist Marija Gimbutas, who called the former Yugoslavia region "the cradle of the spiral." I knew that Almira had not read Gimbutas' research into the Vinča Neolithic period, with its extraordinary artifacts demonstrating a peaceful collective that once prevailed in this war-torn land. Gimbutas investigated the signs and symbols of Neolithic script to determine the ancient meanings and found that the spiral symbol represents the life-death-life cycle aligned with the cycles of life, death, and regeneration[1]. The spiral symbol has been present in South Slavic culture, as if passed down through the blood. I did not tell Almira about this observation, nor did I attempt to layer my textbook knowledge over her immediate, extraordinary moment of manifesting through her actions the power to protect her family. I did share with her that the spiral is an active icon of comfort for many of us, that her spontaneous expression linked her to a larger female family that shares her desire for peace and protection. She nodded in understanding that the spiral was an indigenous, cultural symbol to South Slavs.

Almira shared the memories of the grandmothers she had thought were lost to her forever. As she etched the spiral on her swollen belly, she created

1 M. Gimbutas, (1989). *The language of the goddess.* San Francisco: Harper & Row.

As she etched the spiral on her swollen belly, she created a new social memory, one that recalled the intergenerational a new social memory, one that recalled the intergenerational wisdom of her grandmothers and Neolithic ancestors. For a few precious minutes, she severed her maternal fright. I thought of my responsibility as a mother and elder, recalling times when I had failed to foster an environment for gestation, birth, and growth. I had left those spaces to be filled with maternal fright.

As I continued to work in Bosnia, I began to recognize the plethora of stories of maternal fright. One story was repeated to me several times, each by different individuals. As the story was repeated, different aspects emerged, as if each teller layered on her individual symbolic message that had gone unheeded through a century of wars. For me, the story demarcates the extreme extent of the term *horror*. I witnessed the way memory is seared into our brains, embedded in our complex neurological network and bound by fright and horror. And I have seen the trauma of a grandmother reappear generations later.

I cannot name a more effective way to instill fear into the masses of humanity and all living beings than that borne from maternal fright narratives. I must appeal to you now; please tell me what to do with the story of an infant baked in the oven during the Ahmica war crimes massacre. How do any of us handle that knowledge without succumbing to the trauma of horror? While it is here in this book, and writing it down has helped me to channel the horror through myself and give birth to the story I carry through these pages, it is still haunting to all who hear and now read about the tragedy. In part, I fear that in repeating it, I continue the manmade intergenerational trauma instead of passing on intergenerational wisdom.

All but one who spoke of the story were female. The females spoke of the home, one's place of comfort, as a central part of the horror, adding to the trauma by its very nature. Each told the story with similar emphasis on the phrases, "right in the home, *her* house, *her* oven." It is true that the surviving female members of that Ahmica household continue to bake food daily in the same oven. They would not survive without their *pech*, their oven, and their bioculinary arts, such as herbal medicines and food remedies that keep them healthy and alive.

In the repeated narrative of the murdered infant, revenge occupies one silent space; none of the women spoke of prejudice against their Croatian neighbors. Not one word of hatred was uttered against those who perpetuated the Balkan war crimes, and no woman advocated for the Croatians to be hated or feared. The story told from the male perspective, however, suggested to the listener that

wisdom of her grandmothers and Neolithic ancestors.

all Croats were evil, ready to kill at a moment's notice. The stark difference in coping suggests that when something is so horrifying that we simply cannot understand it or even create a space for it in our minds, we retreat to our intergenerational wisdom to help us cope. It appears that women, drawing on the memories of their grandmothers, tend to focus on those who are still alive, planning physical

Ahmica-Vitez war crimes survivors

and spiritual nourishment to sustain them. Men, however, move from incomprehension to hatred and prejudice. The space for understanding cannot accommodate such horror as the death of this infant, and each gender is therefore plunged into their automatic, and opposite, reactions.

The women who shared the infant's story were shocked by the targeting of the home, the symbolic womb, the horrible violation of the home that took place as this child was killed. All of the women spoke of being unable to wish this upon any other mother, regardless of whether she was Croat, Serb, or Muslim. For these women, the inability to comprehend how anyone could do such a thing becomes another insight. With their awareness that all things feminine were the target of aggression and violence came a universal consciousness that prompted female solidarity. What I noted was their assertion that *any* mother would reel under the horror that the family in that violated home experienced.

The home—the womb—is the ultimate intentional target for the male warrior, from individual violence to military campaigns. Due to the feminine capacity to manifest culture and bear and raise children, war itself is founded on the principle that the life of the enemy should be exterminated and that this is best accomplished by targeting women. I think of the bombing of London and Dresden in WWII and the release of the first nuclear bomb on Hiroshima. The term *civilian causalities* essentially refers to the annihilation of the enemy by removing female genealogies. This is why soldiers rape mothers and target their sons on the battlefield.

I think of Joan Hinton, a physicist who joined the Maoist revolution after helping develop atomic weapons in the Manhattan Project. Living on a farm in China and raising cows and other livestock, she went on to live the life-death-life spiral, rejecting mass killing. Hinton once said, "I don't want to spend my life figuring out how to kill people."[2] She went on to live her life in the same fashion as the Ahmica war crimes survivors, following the pattern

2 B. Gintis. (2007). *Engaging the movement of life*. North Atlantic Books.

The sulfurous fumes of maternal fright and the Ahmica women's war crime stories swirled in the ubiquitous cigarette smoke.

of Neolithic self-sustainability in their crops and chickens by manifesting peaceful culture in daily living practices.

During each of my journeys to Bosnia, the Sumejja Kolo women arranged for a meeting. In working with them, I was constantly reminded of the Ahmica women's labors on the land as they fed and milked the cows that helped sustain their families. During my visit in 2003, arrangements were made so that I spent one night in Ahmica with a woman named Nemana, whose house stood next the mosque that had been destroyed in the Balkan War.

That evening, Nemana barely spoke to me. She eyed me through the smoke as she consumed a pack of cigarettes in less than two hours. I was choking and my eyes ran as I watched her make cheese in her kitchen sink. I had never seen the process before and told her that the curds looked like vomit. I thought she was going to slap me. I laughed as she shook her head and released an expletive about "stupid Americans." I retorted that "stupid Bosnians smoked like chimneys in the house," and we both laughed. This moment showed me that we would get along well, despite our differences; we trusted each other enough to tease about nationality, which seemed to be a treacherous subject in this war-damaged town that sat so close to its former enemies.

She, a grandmother Nemana began to share her process for making cheese. I was eager to share more heightened experiences with her and learn from her wisdom. was sharing with me, a mother, a bioculinary process for making cheese. Nemana told me that her favorite cow made the best cheese. She explained that this cow ate particular grasses, flowers, and herbs so that her cheese had a hint of these healing flavors. That cow had been killed during the war. She did not share any details about her beloved cow's death, and I knew not to ask since I wanted to honor the space between the cigarette smoking when we shared a resonant silence.

I told Nemana that I had no idea where I could put a cow on my land at home, and she shook her head while gleefully lighting another cigarette. She scolded me for coughing around her cheese, and I pretended to retaliate. She laughed. During the sharing of the cheese process, she told me that her daughter-in-law and grandson live upstairs. Pulling the cheese cloth from her handmade kitchen cabinet, she reported that her son works far away and comes home only occasionally.

Nemana's house had been rebuilt after the war, but not on the same foundation. I asked her what happened to the original foundation. She told me that instead of planting her garden around the entire perimeter of the rebuilt house, she used the home's original, pre-war foundation for her garden. Nemana was bringing new life to her home. Dragging on her cigarette, she told me that I knew nothing about paying homage to ancestors in order to understand how they died. I hung my head and said that I felt fortunate not to know.

I was thinking of the fresh corn and Bosnian *salata* filled with cucumbers, white onions, and tomatoes that came from the very garden that Nemana planted where her home had once stood. I admired her resiliency and ability to nourish her family in the ashes of war. I began to cry, not from the cigarette smoke but from the realization that I was eating a meal grown on the very land on which my own ancestors were killed. Nemana sensed the emotion that had inspired an altogether new shape of our conversation and caused my stream of tears. Her powerful perception fostered a special state of presence between us, which forged a lasting bond.

Nemana & her grandson standing on the same path she ran from genocide

The riot of neurochemicals streaming through my body from facing trauma and maternal fright followed me into Nemana's guest bedroom that night, as I felt the geophysical peculiarities of complete darkness one can only experience in a rural area. The sulfurous fumes of maternal fright and the Ahmica women's war crime stories swirled in the ubiquitous cigarette smoke. I could hear the green magic marker scrawl a spiral and the drip of my tears in the pitch-dark bedroom. Strangely, I felt cleansed but not purified. I went straight into a coma-like sleep.

During the cheese-making, Nemana spoke of the loss of her children and grandchildren. She added that the loss of her neighbors had also felt like the loss of family. The cigarette haze swirled as she shared her memories of neighbors who had nurtured her in moments of need. The next morning, she invited her neighbor, a lifelong friend, to share more impossibly difficult stories of carnage. I clapped my hands over my ears as the two neighbors shared story after story. I pulled in all of my skills to bear witness to a load that I knew I could never hold.

REFLECTIONS

The retelling of war crimes taught me the lesson of male anger, displaced aggression, and horrific violence as it becomes amplified through a series of war events. Worse than male aggression, however, is the lasting impact of intergenerational memories of trauma that are fueled by maternal fright. The pregnant Ahmica mother Almira instructed me primarily in victimhood, which will always need an offender.

In reciprocal fashion, my bearing witness instructed them about their martyr-like presence. As I wept and declared that I could not bear witness to much more and held onto all that they were teaching, I offered in return a lesson about martyrdom. Within every martyr is the need to be superior to the offender, to rise above him through forgiveness and healing. As victims, women are immediately prescribed into the martyr role, perpetuating intergenerational trauma so that it is inscribed more deeply into the future.

The experiences of the total immersion in the destruction of female genealogies and war crimes further augmented my understanding of medical and neurological studies on the impact of maternal fright on gestating mothers and the unborn. German embryologist Erich Blechschmidt's research on the embryologic development of the beginning stages of pregnancy, the ten- to fifteen-day period when the brain's anterior midline is forged, shows that, "the process is guided by motion, motion relationships, metabolic field, fluid dynamics, and a precision that is epigenetic, not dictated by a genetic code."[3] In other words, the mother's body interacts with the fetus, potentially shaping development as a result of the mother's emotional experiences. If the mother resides in fear, fear will present a formidable obstacle for the future generation, who may experience an increase in mental health disorders as a result. We are reminded that trauma is psychobiological.

Essentially, the traumatic stories seemed to have the ability to make women sterile or perhaps to etch upon the eggs in our wombs a host of genetic diseases and the propensity for intergenerational trauma. Eradicating intergenerational trauma is simple. Engagement and support of young and gestating mothers while creating a safe, healthy environment is all that is needed. We can all participate in this on the ground floor level, becoming a collective across the globe with each small act.

---

3 B. Gintis. (2007). *Engaging the movement of life.* North Atlantic Books. p. 127.

Erin Hilleary

CHAPTER 4

Ethnochoreology

WHERE AND WHEN I BORE WITNESS

From 1999 to 2010, I witnessed the kolo danced by the women of Novi Travnik, Bosnia. There are many ways to dance the kolo that do not follow its typical representation of undulating bodies and feet pounding the floor of the earth to the rhythm of the violin, goat skin pipes, and accordion. The most memorable kolos are the silent kolos of the Srebrenica widows as they sat at their looms weaving rugs, or *kilims*, in Tuzla, Republic of Serbia.

Tuzla was once a part of Bosnia, but the Dayton Peace Agreement changed the geographic boundaries. Signed during the Christian holiday season in Paris on December 14, 1995, the Dayton Peace Agreement was written to preserve the state of Bosnia. However, the Agreement caused the division of the war-torn land; 51% of Bosnia's territory was shared by the Croats and Muslims, and 49% became the Serbian Republic. This division increased the people's suffering in the aftermath of war and the war crimes that were perpetrated by the neighboring Serb military. More than 200,000 people died in the three-and-a-half-year war. A further estimated 3 million refugees flooded into Europe, bringing with them reminders of the haunting, ghastly images of suitcase refugees from WWI and WWII.

I continued to witness, through the Ahmica war survivors and Novi Travnik Kolo Sumejja women, how words on paper can seed violence and war and trigger intergenerational revenge. That revenge stems from the source of trauma that is passed into future generations through unresolved hatred.

STORIED INSTRUCTIONS

Near Mount Vranica, a river once sprang from the mountainside near a series of caves called the Angel Caves. The trees bordered the river's edge and rocks sat happily under the cascading water, effortlessly spilling into the valleys of the Bosnian landscape. One night in 1937, that river disappeared.

The only evidence that this river ever existed is the now dry, rocky riverbed and the trees whose roots reach longingly for the water that once fed them. The Angel Caves nearby remain unexplored. The Disappearing River has become a symbol—a message—to the Bosnian people, which they cite to this day. Its ominous nature is perhaps the reason why those caves remain undisturbed. Back in 1937, the local people knew that the river's disappearance foretold war, famine, and death.

During the Balkan War, the Angel Caves had housed weapons and soldiers. The Novi Travnik mountaineers[1] explored the caves with little equipment and spoke of

1 Medex Mine Awareness, a Bosnian-Herzegovinian non-profit that teaches children how to survive landmines, is run by the Novi Travnik mountaineers, a group of men who survived the Balkan War. The Novi Travnik mountaineers performed rescue missions in the mountains and caves.

attempted rescues within the Angel Caves, where bodies were lost and never recovered. The Bosnian mountaineers were mostly young males who traveled with older, more seasoned males who led the rescue operations. During the war, the mountaineers were the best soldiers, trained to survive the harsh alpine environment by finding shelter in the wilderness.

The ancient South Slavic wise women would have interpreted the river's disappearance and the mysterious Angel Caves as signs of the great *troika*, the life-death-life spiral—an example of the ultimate ethnochoreology. The term *ethnochoreology* comes from the prefix *ethno-*, meaning people and culture, and the base word *choreograph*, which refers to the pattern of a dance routine or the organization of dance movements, along with a focus on organization, coordination, and supervision of the event. Choreology is a system in which any form or pattern of movements and dance are documented. The South Slavs interpreted natural events through analogous human movements, and the act of reading the signs from Mother Nature remains a critical part of their lives. Dancing the kolo is not just the act of performing a dance; it is the reenactment of the very cycle of life.[2]

According to Jungian psychology's teleological approach, signs and messages have meaning and purpose.[3] These signs are "ingested" implicitly (i.e., internally through memory), as well as explicitly (i.e., externally through somatic movements, such as those induced by the kolo). The life-death-life spiral sign represents life experience that must be acknowledged before it can institute awareness or insight. The South Slavic oral tradition is steeped in memory practices that are inclusive of body and mind, through which symbolic and iconic messages are ingested and interpreted into patterns. These patterns allow a culture to organize its rituals and traditions. Since they are inclusive of both mind and body, we identify ethnochoreology as an invaluable process for Slavs.

Also, biosemiotic in nature the somatic movements of the kolo and circle attests to our social life from time immemorial as a world of culture and as a world of nature. Breaking down the term biosemiotic, we have bio-life and semiotics which are signs and meaning that exist in all living systems. Therefore, what we call biosemiotic and mapped by ethnochoreology is the deep parallel of our genetic code, using the symbolic language, as old as life itself through danced hieroglyphics, is but a living language. While invisible our genetic code is buried in the cavernous cells of our bodies become visible with ethnochoreology and its poetic metaphor.

Rivers that ceased to flowed, soaking through into the earth, suggested to the Bosnian people that life had gone underground, a foretelling of the *end of days*. Like the bodies that were never found in the Angel Caves, the river had disappeared and had never been traced again. Many Bosnians searched their oral history and myth narratives to find an explanation for the river's disappearance. The local people tell a new mythic narrative to describe the river's silent vanishing; they say a silent kolo was danced while they slept, and it was then that the river stopped flowing.

2 For more information on the Kolo as somatic movement and psychological healing, http://www.kolocollaboration.org/?item=20098

3 Diamond, J., & Jones, L. S. (2004). A path made by walking: Process work in practice. Portland, Oregon: Lao Tse Press.

The round dance, with its circle format, provides an avenue through which trauma is healed and ethnochoreological practices are perpetuated. South Slavic cuisine and culinary arts are also a part of the kolo oral memory tradition and are often accompanied by a rich, thick demitasse of Bosnian coffee. The small cup, once emptied of its coffee, is turned over to dry the thick coffee grounds that remain. The thick grounds, like tea leaves, are read by the women for signs and symbols. The kolo and the cup readings shift between trance states within everyday consciousness, dealing with unbearable pain and loss. It was during the kolo meeting and reading of coffee cups that I discovered the vital link that connects the symbols, signs, and hidden messages with the meaning that underlies the extreme pain and loss experienced by war survivors.

On the day of my visit in Tuzla, each of the Srebrenica widows had revealed the same messages in their coffee grounds: guns and graves[4]. I was stunned that the little granules in the bottom of their cups were so uniform in meaning that I was at a loss for words. I reflected on the widows' cup readings and the river's mysterious disappearance. The symbolism for both translated into war and death. That day, we shared a silence of understanding, a silence that reminded us of our shared ancient history.

4 For more on signs and cup readings, see http://www.kolocollaboration.org/?item=16982

After my trauma treatment sessions with the Srebrenica widows of Tuzla, I traveled home on the bus with my companions, the women of the Kolo Sumejja. The Srebrenica women had shared their stories with us as they weaved their kilims at Bosfam, a humanitarian organization run by the local women who survived war crimes. Throughout our return trip from Tuzla to Novi Travnik, we remained silent. I vividly recall this silence as it captured the traumatic aftermath of our visit with the widows; we were silenced, unable to put into words our profound feelings of empathy, our vocabularies unable to sufficiently describe the trauma. The horrifying accounts of rape, assault, and murder left a strained atmosphere around us as we empathetically bore the weight of those embattled women. On that bus, we danced a silent kolo, a round dance that acted out our search for expression.

The name *Srebrenica* means *made of silver*, a name given to the region for its local mines and caverns. As I looked about the tattered yellow and green bus while the Kolo Sumejja women and I danced the silent kolo, I reflected upon the caverns we passed through that never saw a ray of sunshine, with no hope of words or expression to be found. Ironically,

Sana Koric standing and Vahdeta Sivro Krnic

the very place no sunlight could penetrate produced flashing silver metals almost as bright as the full moon. I prayed for words to convey the experience of sitting shoulder-to-shoulder with the Srebrenica war crimes widows.

The Kolo Sumejja women and I feared the breaking of our transcendent silence almost as much as we feared dealing with the aftermath of violence. It is no wonder that people avoid entering the silence, because it obliges us to seek the profound without the use of words to mitigate its effect. Too often, we fill silence with chatter, busy work, heavy schedules, and service to all else except ourselves.

The debilitating fear that settled over our yellow and green bus signified our learning as we began to gain wisdom and insight. We allowed our fear to point us to silence, a way to learn from catastrophic events. Without instruction or discussion, we synchronized our realities; we looked together into the silent past and began to understand how to heal the present.

I learned from the Srebrenica war crimes widows that the entirety of past memories, especially those of war crimes, offers silence as a gateway into the profound where words are unnecessary and, perhaps, even detrimental. I had to remove my expectation that I would hear sentiments of hatred spewing from the women's mouths. Rather than calls for retribution or shame, the widows spoke of gratitude for having survived and for gaining knowledge and understanding along the way. The gratitude might have stemmed from the dance of the women's fingers on their looms. Designing brightly colored kilims together, with an ethnochoreology that defies logic and transcends trauma, seemed so mysterious to me, laden with infinite possibilities. The weaving of kilims flows as mysteriously as the river that disappeared in 1937.

The Bosnian kilims are filled with signs and symbols that are shaped similarly to the 6,500- to 8,000-year-old Old European Danube scripts. Yet, the Srebrenica women had never finished school, learned to drive, nor worked outside of their homes; they had never read books filled with those ancient inscriptions. Rather, the widows demonstrate that the past is filled with memories that pass from one generation to the next, static in nature as they flow from mothers to daughters and remain preserved in handmade artifacts. The Srebrenica widows are creating the future as they draw on the past; the ethnochoreology that is embedded in their kilims allows them to weave their grief into a herstory that will teach future generations about survival and community. With each kilim, the widows weave ancient memories into new patterns, creating and recreating herstory. Their creative acts through the simple loom will live on long after their deaths. In an ironic parallel, trauma victims who exhibit post-traumatic stress disorder (PTSD) often relive the tormenting memories as vividly as they had originally occurred.

Bosfam Advocacy project

It is with a heavy heart that I admit I can no longer visit the Srebrenica Bosfam widows with the Kolo Sumejja women from Novi Travnik. My Bosnian Serb father was born just outside of Tuzla in a small village named Turijak, though his village no longer exists. My father was expelled by the Croatian-born leader Tito. After WWII, Winston Churchill sided with Tito, a more dashing figure than the poor peasant workers who made up the guerilla outfit known as the Chetniks. While Novi Travnik and Ahmica have been closely shared by Serbs, Croats, and Muslims, Srebrenica is situated on the outskirts of Tuzla where it is more ethnically isolated. Serbs and Muslims were neighbors and friends in Novi Travnik and Ahmica, and before the Balkan War, many Serbs left Novi Travnik, begging their Muslim neighbors to remember WWII. However, in Srebrenica, Muslims watched Serbian war criminals target and murder their male family members. Even now in the former Yugoslavia, the Chetniks—mostly Serbs—are considered to be the reviled figures in war memorials and media documentaries. Tito remains a beloved hero who is widely credited with keeping peace in the former Yugoslavia for fifty years. The patriotic hero-worship of Tito is a sad commentary on the dangers of propaganda, especially in light of the bloody Balkan Wars of the 1990s. Many question the price of those fifty years of peace, since the silent oppression that characterized those years masked the virulent hatred that led to the outbreak of the Balkan War thus creating a devastating trio of wars over a century.

Tuzla destroyed building with trees

The three times that I accompanied the Kolo Sumejja women to Tuzla to watch the women weave their kilims, I was undeniably branded *an American Serb woman whose father was a Chetnik*. Of course, I could only see that we were all daughters of the same earth facing violence and searching for healing; but, the Srebrenica widows who I had come to witness had seen a much stronger ethnic division than seen by the women of Novi Travnik and Ahmica. Thus, it may be that I cannot adequately describe these experiences, because I have always felt the shadow of the hatred and blood spilled by my father's own hands. Perhaps this is an underlying reason that my life's work has come to offer trauma treatment and therapy for victims of PTSD.

The last time we gathered together as a kolo, I described to the women that we are complicit in violence by failing to say "No" and by relinquishing our inner authority to the patriarchal head of the household. I asked the women to search where female rage had gone—not only in Bosnia but across the globe. Sana Koric, the female head of the Kolo

Sumejja, confessed that she was concerned about my safety after the last meeting with the Srebrenica widows, because I had raised many sensitive subjects.

"I had to make sure they did not have knives waiting for you," she said, half-jokingly. I turned to her as she fumbled for her carton of cigarettes and told her, "Women do not kill in aggression and violence." She immediately agreed, teasing that it was a miracle she had not done so to me. We both laughed, then hugged like sisters, despite the superficial difference between us—the fact that one of us is a Bosnian Muslim and the other is an American Serb.

Sana and the Kolo Sumejja women spoke of an overpowering "Land of They," similar to Americans' imaginary division between "us" and "them." Like the Srebrenica women, though, I was confused, because the Kolo Sumejja had never defined who "they" were, though they often spoke about what "they" had done. Finally, after many sessions with the women, I stood up in the middle of the meeting, and pronounced to the women, somewhat nervously, "I get it." I realized that, whether or not we would ever admit it, "they" are our fathers, husbands, uncles, brothers, cousins, and sons—the men who kill during war. I faced a silence so still and powerful that it seethed and rippled with aggression as opposed to peace. I was nervous in speaking my truth.

REFLECTIONS

The residue of hatred and fear cannot be washed away in a single lifetime. It is reenacted generation after generation if we do nothing to break the cycle, to move through the troika of life-death-life. The Srebrenica widows reawaken a distant vague memory of acts that were perpetrated by previous generations as they grieve at their looms for their lost loved ones. I, too, followed this path. By returning to the birthplace of my father, a man whose war trauma spilled over into post-war life in a new country and threatened to destroy my entire family, I followed the spiral out of trauma into healing and out of death into life.

I gently reminded the Kolo women—from the Kolo Sumejja leader, Sana Koric, to the Srebrenica widows—that their husbands, for whom they mourn, were also soldiers. Their lost loved ones took other lives with them when they died in battle. They left their homes and went to Croatia to kill someone else's son, while the Croatian mother sent her son over here to do the same. The same is true for every soldier's wife or mother. We cannot claim grief for our own and hoard it as if it will make us feel better; we must acknowledge the grief of the "enemy," opening our hearts to the grief that they too feel, before we can truly heal. We cannot walk only one side of the spiral. We cannot heal only half of the trauma. *We cannot dance half of a kolo.*

Do we ever consider how, as Americans, we send our sons, husbands, or fathers to other lands to kill? The guise of patriotism cannot hide what those actions truly are: murder. We must stop assigning euphemisms to murder in our attempts to justify the means to our ends. *Just* ends do not require murderous means.

"I get it," I said to Sana Koric and the Kolo Sumejja women. I told them it would be a long time before I could forgive them for giving me this awareness. In the meantime, I asked them to dance the kolo with me so that I could channel the intense *female rage* into healing the collective communal. You see, I am living with the fact that I am just as complicit in aggression and violence as the men who killed. I am one of those who grieve for the losses of war, and I, too, struggle not to name "them." My father's war wounds and those of my lost relatives burn inside me, alongside my female rage. I channel my anger to saying "no," to refusing to participate in continued anger and aggression, and embrace only in healing.

The repeated immersion in the kolo and the silent kolo has led me to face the truth that we, as mothers, raise our children to be the women and men of the future. Thus, it is our duty to take responsibility for teaching them the just way to be women and men, the just way to forgive and heal, and the just way to honor the humanity within us by allowing it to flourish. Whether our neighbors worship in mosques or pray to patron saints, or even follow no religion at all, we must allow the flame of humanity to burn unhindered. We must become "we," not "us" and "them."

Marko Borkovich Chetnik

Erin Hilleary

CHAPTER 5

Hands & Feet

WHERE AND WHEN I BORE WITNESS

In 2002, the Kolo Sumejja women introduced me to Rasema in Novi Travnik, Bosnia. "She is not doing well, and we need to help somehow," the leader of Kolo Sumejja told me. Large-boned and almost six feet tall, with wide hands and large feet, Rasema lived in a tiny Bosnian house with her sister, who was known for her singing voice. Both Rasema and her sister experienced chronic pain in their legs. Her sister's leg problems had disabled her dramatically in middle age, giving her a significant limp. Rasema's legs kept her from experiencing life without pain. She was mostly seen with her hands tucked into her pockets, unless she was busy cooking or baking fine sheets of phyllo dough filled with cheese or meat. The tiny house in which they lived was situated near a stream that fed the artesian well from which the older women gathered water on a daily basis. Rasema explained to me that it was too far to walk into town, barely a quarter of a mile down the road.

STORIED INSTRUCTIONS

Rasema was widowed twice; she buried her two husbands along with two sons. On our first visit, she gazed down at her large hands and told me, "I buried my husbands and sons with these hands." She was known to sleep on her sons' graves at night in the Muslim graveyard outside Novi Travnik, Bosnia. She peered down and said

"I'd walk there with these feet."

Rasema's second husband was Croat, making her sons and herself a target for both Muslim and Croat hatred, especially from her husband's brother. Imprisoned in their own house during the Balkan War, the Croat military came to deliver the news to Rasema and her husband that their second son had been killed. Shortly after the soldiers left, Rasema's Croat husband took a gun and killed himself. Over the years, I have heard many versions of this story from Rasema and other women; I have learned that the brain layers new memories over our horrific ones so that what we perceive as the truth will fit into our current state of mind and situation.

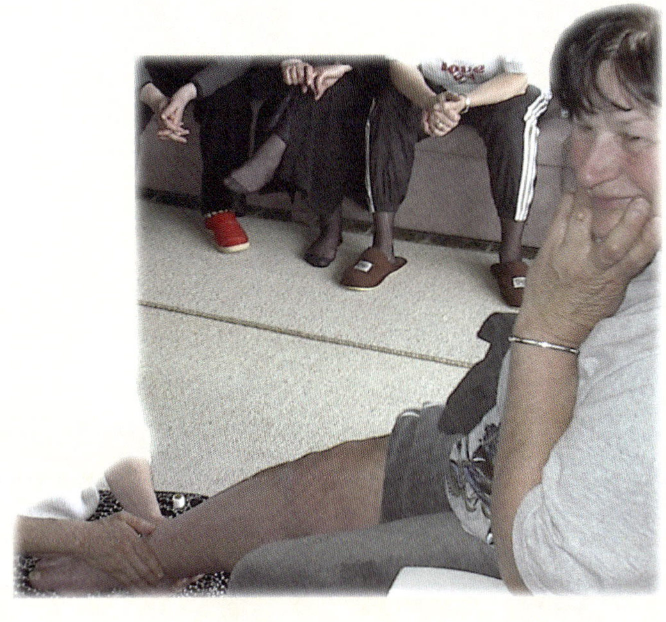

Rasema getting a therapeutic massage.

Rasema taught me how difficult it is for a mother to bury two sons and two

When I inquired about her first husband, Rasema shared with me that he had died from leukemia after serving in the army. Her answer echoed that of many other Muslim women in that region of Bosnia. The countless times I heard this cause of death from Muslim wives seemed too often to be possible. Statistically, the disease would have been beyond the rates of an epidemic. Some believe the common link between the deaths of these Muslim men is blood transfusions they had received; however, no studies have tested this association. Could HIV/ AIDS be the true cause of Rasema's first husband's death and the deaths of so many Bosnian Muslim men in the 1980s and early 1990s?

Ethnic hatred based on religious divides was certainly repressed hatreds for fifty years under Tito's communist rule[1]. Rasema spoke of the hatred her husband's brother and nephew had had for Rasema and her son. I searched her face and body and wondered how anyone could tell if she was Croat, Muslim, or Serb. Certainly, color was not an issue; we are all Caucasian. Nor do I think it was solely religion that deepened the divide; rather, there is a vulnerability in the way religion penetrates and controls the indigenous culture that women create in their daily lives. In other words, while women struggle to nourish and nurture their families, religion bends those practices into rituals and dogmas that reinforce a biased view, one with divisions between brothers and violence among neighbors.

I witnessed a true example of this when the Kolo Sumejja women took me to visit Jayce, now a Croat- controlled city. "Don't call out our first names, Danica," implored the women. I realized that my experiences had not prepared me to face the variety of emotional and biological targets for ethnic hatred that are familiar to the Kolo Sumejja women. Calling out their names, as I often do while cupping my hands around my mouth like a mini megaphone to gain their attention, would let their Islamic first names fall upon Croat ears. And perhaps, according the Kolo Sumejja women, this would cause their hands and those of Croats to commit violence. I did not want to test out that theory.

Rasema, with a fixed and intent stare into my eyes, gripped my arm with her large hands and spoke in loud whispers after I asked about her son. She told me about her stepson, her second husband's son from his previous marriage; he (the stepson) "was there when my son was killed. The army said they were playing roulette, but I know [my son's uncle and cousin] had wanted to kill him for years." I searched her face for any hatred or malice. I found only a mother's sorrow at not being able to protect her son from her stepson and for decisions that, once made, set the course of fate.

The stepson and his father, Rasema's brother-in-law wanted all Bosnian Muslims killed. Hatreds do not die but others die. Rasema's marriage to a Croat (Catholic) and her being Muslim set the stage for killing.

Rasema taught me how difficult it is for a mother to bury two sons and two husbands, none of whom died from natural causes. The other women told me that Rasema did not want the dirt to be poured over her sons' coffins; her

1 Josip Broz Tito was chief architect of the second Yugoslavia, a socialist federation that lasted from WWII until 1991.

husbands, none of whom died from natural causes.

hands begged to dig out the earth. To this day, she still has not accepted the deaths of her sons, but perpetuates her own victimhood as she refuses to surrender to her grief.

As we talked during our treatment sessions, I could see Rasema modeling through acceptance the depth of the mother-child bond. Acceptance is relentless and ever-changing. It is no small feat to face acceptance when we are trapped in the role of martyred women. We must move away from victimhood and supersede those who victimize us. Most women do not know how to surrender to life; they see it as a linear progression from the cradle to the grave. South Slavs, however, understand the troika of life-death-life and know that we often move from life into death and back into life as we heal from our trauma. Rasema was battling against acceptance of her grief and surrendering to the surging life around her. Why would she walk back into her life after the deaths of her sons and second husband? I still ask myself, "Is this the reason for the pain in her legs and back? Does she carry her grief physically, recalling it anew with each painful step toward the graves of her family?"

Not knowing how to approach the abyss of depression that trapped Rasema in her cycle of relentless, repetitive behaviors, I searched the academic world—my clinical books, psychological studies, and celebrated therapy modalities—for a technique that could guide us in the feminine sense of lived experiences. I found none. I knew from my own mother's and father's survival of WWII and from the concentration camps that South Slavs can remain locked in this condition for generations; just as we can pass on intergenerational wisdom through our blood, so can we pass on intergenerational trauma. Intergenerational trauma is the epigenetic process shaping our genes and environment. How could we heal women like Rasema recover instead of remaining stuck in her painful cycle of grief? How could I cover the wide range of awareness borne from catastrophic and holocaustic events that women alone experience?

I dismissed any agenda or timeline and waited for a propitious moment to present itself. At one of our gatherings with Rasema, I told her in no uncertain terms that I could not sleep on the cold graves with her. Rasema jerked her hands up, saying that she would never ask me to do so. Because shame for a South Slavic woman is the failure to be an extraordinary hostess, my challenge struck a chord with Rasema. I stood my ground and said that if I came to visit her at night, she would not be home since I would see her along the way sleeping on her sons' graves. I pointed out that, in this case, I would have to visit her at the grave site and sleep there. I was unsure whether I had jolted her from her grief with my *food for thought*, not sure if my suggestion would lead to healing or if I had mortally offended her. I stepped back and grabbed for Sana, the leader of Kolo Sumejja, to protect me. The Kolo women were taken completely off guard by the moment that I had created. Instead of the damage I feared, laughter erupted, as opposed to a slap from Rasema's wide Slavic hands. Rasema laughed until she cried. I am not sure if the tears were from laughter or grief. Perhaps I instigated her begin the healing process by pushing her slightly away from the

One Kolo Sumejja mother from Novi Travnik, Bosnia, pointed out that Rasema at least had a grave to visit; many women

spiral of depression in which she walked to and from her sons' graves. Her negative spiral, always leading back to death, could become a positive spiral, bringing life.

As Rasema's tears dried, she looked down at me and called me *pametna* (meaning *smart* or *smart aleck*). I am not entirely sure which she meant, but the most important outcome was that Rasema stopped sleeping on the graves since she never knew when I would come to visit. Rasema joked at later Kolo Sumejja gatherings about what it would look like to have an American Serb woman sleeping on Muslim graves. That time, I laughed until I cried. During that meeting, Rasema washed her face, her hands dripping with tears of laughter, not sorrow. She got up on her feet to serve me another heaping plate of squash pita, a handmade strudel she had lovingly made.

The Kolo Sumejja women coaxed Rasema to talk and to become more active in our kolo meetings. Rasema slowly moved away from depression as she moved closer to the group. Coaxing Rasema out of the cave pits of her depression was no small feat. I marveled at how the Kolo Sumejja women healed trauma with no funding or materials, only the wisdom of their life experiences and that of their mothers before them. The way the Bosnian women did this was through the daily, random practice of dropping by for thick Bosnian coffee during both day and night. Rasema, the quintessential hostess, would jump off the sofa positioned near the television, usually blaring a western movie, to prepare coffee and food.

Often, the women would scold her for sleeping on the sofa rather than the bed. We all secretly preferred this practice to her sleeping on her family's graves. One Kolo Sumejja mother from Novi Travnik, Bosnia, pointed out that Rasema at least had a grave to visit; many women could only hold vigil at Cavkarka Kod Trusine, known as the cave pits. The Muslims of the former Yugoslavia had suffered greatly during WWII under General Draza Mihailovic, leader of King Peter's Royal Armed Forces, and from the tyranny of Chetniks, a radical Serbian Orthodox guerilla war pack who followed orders to cleanse Bosnia of the so-called cancer of Islam. The terror campaign raped the women, executed male Muslims, and threw their bodies into the cave pits with smashed skulls.[1]

The way in which the Kolo Sumejja mothers had so clearly remembered the WWII terror campaign and cave pits reminded me of the South Slavic ability to recite thousands of lines of ancient poetry, the capacity to pass memory through the generations. Just as scops and bards recited epics like Beowulf around the fire in civilizations that relied on oral tradition to pass on stories and history, South Slavs continue to carry the patterns and rhythms that their ancestors used to keep their tales alive.

The Balkan War in the 1990s repeated the practice of the cave pits from WWII. I noted that the Muslim women war survivors regarded burial as one last

2 Retrieved from http://worldupdates.tripod.com/islamintheworld/id23.htm

could only hold vigil at Čavkarka Kod Trusine, known as the cave pits.

place of dignity and honor, which shows us how degrading and dehumanizing these cave pits were intended to be. They were planned as both a final and ongoing degradation for the survivors to face, a continued trauma that reinforced the brutality of war. The troika consciousness is never erased in South Slavs, not even for those who emigrate, like my family and me. I considered the plasticity of the troika in the context of Rasema's life events. In this way, I share Rasema's grief, both learning from her wisdom and lightening her burden, and I then see the cave pits and the graves of Rasema's sons in a new light. I experience the troika; I walk through death and back into life. Rasema, too, walked with painful steps to her son's graves, but she also walked back to her home and prepared food for her friends, all the while continuing to open up within the circle of the kolo. Rasema's hands were soon free to scoop coffee grounds to brew comfort for her healing circle of women, leaving the ground that covers her sons in place.

Rasema's daughter survived the war and immigrated to the States. Rasema had refused to leave the graves of her husband and sons at first, but she soon gained the strength to visit her daughter. She had felt as if she was abandoning her sons. She feared that if she had chosen to live in America, she would lose her culture, thereby losing even more contact with and protection of her buried loved ones. She told me that she had already forgotten ways in which she would midwife life and how to dance the kolo. Her legs constantly pained her, as she had not completely migrated through the landscapes of acceptance and surrender at our last encounter. Only Rasema will know when her mourning is finished.

THE IMPACT

I waited and learned to bear witness to Rasema's journey through trauma and mourning. She had to first, however, traverse and survive the morphing fields of depression. The term *morph* comes from Greek, meaning to take on different shapes and forms. This shape-shifting bled

Rasema 41 White Beans Biosemiotic oral memory traditions

into mental and body habitual behaviors which caused Rasema's depression to look like grief, though it was merely the remnants of that grief being kept alive through her continual focus on the deaths in her past.

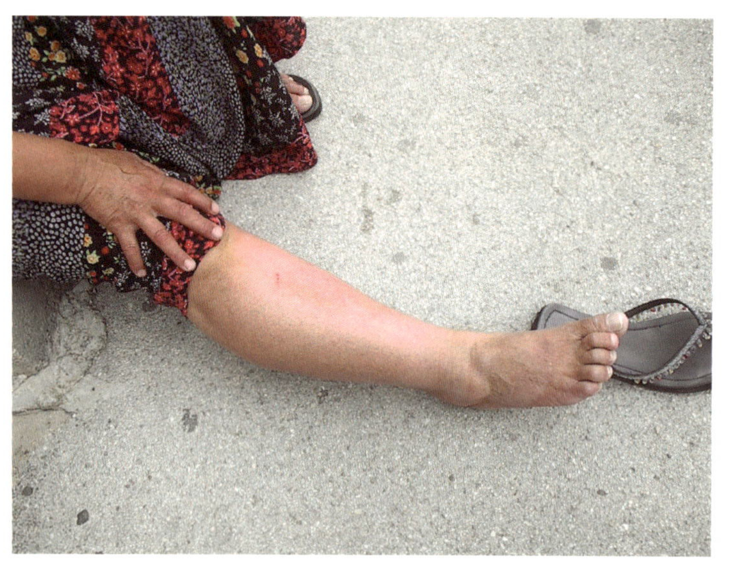

Rasema, as my professor of collective anguish, tapped directly into archetypal creation forces and acts. Whatever form her depression took, whether it was the loop she walked to the grave sites or the physical pain in her legs, Rasema was too comfortable with the raw powerful emotions in which she drowned and the sucking mire of martyred motherhood. She was too comfortable in the familiar ruts of life and simply forewent the possibilities of archetypal creative on forces and the behaviors that could bring life back to her.

South Slavic hands and feet are a symbol in and of themselves. Many Slavic sports stars are noted for their large hands and feet, which allow them to excel in the physical arena. Rarely, however, are the hands and feet of Slavic women regarded as anything more than their implements as beasts of burden. The same traits that allow Slavic men to garner praise for their athletic ability serve as symbols of service in their mothers and sisters. These women, relegated to subservient positions, then become prime victims of crimes such as rape and abuse. This treatment is, however, all that the women, their mothers, and their grandmothers have ever known. Imprisoned in tightly focused addiction to daily life, as opposed to the Slavic troika of life-death-life, Slavic women are often oblivious to offers of help or escape and so continue hurtling down the path of a deadened, rut-filled life. How do I keep bearing witness to them and to you? How do I break them out of the self-contained, habitual rut in which passive existence remains in its deadly, motionless grip?

Erin Hilleary

CHAPTER 6

Bogumile

WHERE AND WHEN I BORE WITNESS:

Since March 1999, my journeys to Novi Travnik, Bosnia, have constantly revealed scenery populated by aimless, jobless males loitering the small town's streets. Unemployed Bosnian Muslim males line the Novi Travnik streets on the Bosnian Muslim district side. Just a street away is the very posh Euro Croat neighborhood, with coffee costing perhaps five times as much. Since many cannot afford the cafes for coffee, standing around with nothing to do results in a particular posture: hands stuffed in pockets, while the women bustle past with the children, or perhaps they have potatoes to plant or, if they are fortunate, jobs to go to. Strangely and eerily, the cafés are filled with mostly males and thick smoke.

STORIED INSTRUCTIONS:

The women rushing by with thick waists like tree trunks, wide bags of food, or sacks of potatoes, flour, or kindling, are exhausted from cleaning up after the third of war in one hundred years. The women's bodies look like walking trees to visitors who sweep their eyes across the streets. The jobless and often homeless men stand in the posture of truncated trees—trees that have been felled, deemed worthless, and left to rot.

A young Bosnian males who "bravely" fought in the war, reminds his listeners loudly of his "patriotism," acknowledges that he does not know what to do with all of his warrior skills. Domestic violence reigns in Bosnia as a result of these men, trained to fight but now without an enemy, especially since many consider violence a Bosnian male's cultural right. Calling military skills a cultural right and setting those warriors free in the domestic sphere obliterates the rights of women and children completely, in particular when violence is excused as a "cultural inheritance." The males demonstrate an often stunned and stunted inability to learn from the insanity of holocaustic wars and catastrophic violence, but they nonetheless frequently demand assistance and decry their post-war state.

I am known by the men of Novi Travnik as "the person to talk our stories to." I asked the brave patriotic Bosnian male,

Novi Travnik town center- unemployed men standing in the street

who was in his mid-thirties and whom I smelled long before he stood before me, why people call me that. He shrugged and dragged on his stub of a cigarette; when he exhaled, his sour breath mingled with the thin cigarette smoke. I moved beside him, placing my shoulder beside his shoulder, so that we faced the horizon together. He asked if I was getting prepared to dance the kolo with my move, but I said "no." "It's because you leave and come back months later; you don't live here all the time," stated the Bosnian patriot.

The vast territory to be covered before we can change the Bosnian male view of violence as his cultural right cannot reach the point of transition, the "null point" between two sides of the same coin, as long as the cult of the male remains strong in Bosnia. The head and tail of the coin represent the male and female to me; here in Bosnia, one side is always up, and perhaps it is time to flip the coin. I hardly can take on the feminine psychic makeup as I work with female war survivors and then, when I am asked to listen to men's stories, help him maintain his position as an "entitled male," the very position that keeps the women I work with in the grip of their trauma. Then, in my struggle not to judge or retreat, I thought like a mother; he could be my son. He could be my brother. At this point, I yearned for the Bogumile male that resides in South Slavs, a spiritual guide offering clarity and peace for the protection of all living things. We sat for hours discussing the Bogumiles. I never saw him again after that day, but I have seen him time and again in the many Bosnian men
I speak in an effort to help them heal and rebuild, men who brutally beat their wives and then leave calmly for a day of work.

Another Bosnian male I spoke to, a Croat (if that matters at all), told me of his impotence, reluctantly admitting to me that he knew it was tied to the violence he perpetrated against women during the war. He resisted sleep because sleep deprivation was better than the nightmares in which he relived the horrors of the war each night. His extraordinary state of sleeplessness made him question the purpose of war itself. He wanted to know what patriotism really was and why a country worth fighting for would espouse the kind of violence that he had seen and been urged to commit. I remind him of the South Slavic legend that Jesus gave the Bogumiles the keys to hell. He took this in and asked if I was talking about the *Vrag* (devil in Serbo-Croatian). Somewhere in his past, he studied the Bogumiles, so we were able to discuss thc origins of the *Vrag* legend, which pre-date the Greek Pan, the Sufi wanderer, and the goblin of the night.

Bogumile Standing Stone, Warrior with spiral in one hand to show no weapons

He described his sleeplessness like the goblin of the night, desperately trying to relieve himself of the responsibility for what he had done by saying that the goblin caused his nightmares. I was reminded that the legend of the vampire originated near this region, and I drew a connection in my own mind between the life he had taken from others and the life that he was losing each night as his body was worn down by lack of sleep.

St. George's Day, celebrated on May 6th, may have its roots in the Paleolithic era's fertility rituals; the ancient dances around the phallic tree trunk mirror modern Maypole dances. The strong connections between Catholic, Muslim, and Orthodox beliefs wove their way to the forefront of my interactions with Bosnian male warriors. Legend says that St. George, an Orthodox Christian saint, took ownership of the keys to hell from Jesus.

The Serbian Orthodox Church has a full calendar of *Slava,* which are arranged on various ordained saints. The ancient practice of Slava, family patron saints for South Slavic peoples is a result of their conversion from the Moist Mother Earth based religion to Christianity. The Sufi wanderer is tied the Muslim religion. Jesus is associated here most strongly with the Catholic Church, since the Bogumiles in the 10th century were killed by the pope for not believing in Jesus's divinity.

The root of the word "patriotism" suggests the sweeping father sky god of early nomadic peoples. The Indo-Europeans, Kurgans, and Aryans ended the peaceful Proto-Slavic Neolithic way of life centered in "Old Europe." Patriotism is a pseudo-partnership, if we can even call it a partnership. Joanna Hubbs researched the Northern Slavs' feminine metaphysical pagan ways for her book *Mother Russia* and found them to be a "continuing divinity to associate Her [Mother Earth] with pagan holy trees and water.[1] She stands with her arms raised in a circle – source of all power that united heaven and earth." The natural symbols reflecting matter, the earth, and Goddess show Mother Nature's partnership between male and female not as two sides of a coin but as a continuum in which the health of one depends on the other.

The decimation of great ancient forests and sacred groves eradicated much of the Slavic Mother Tongue, because it is composed of the Mother Nature vocabulary that reveals the kinship of all living matter. Without the original materials from which icons and words were derived, the language becomes barren and loses much of its meaning.

1 Joanna Hubbs, *ibid., p104*

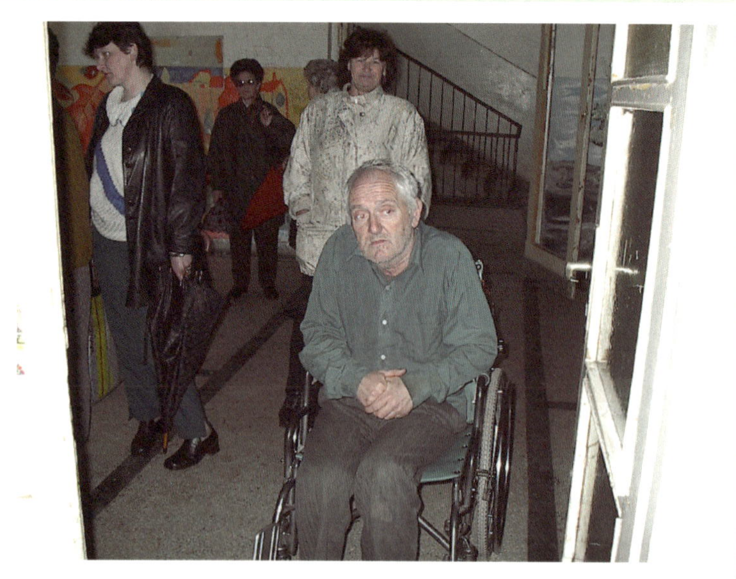

Refugee 10 years later living in an abandoned gymnasium

The Slavic Mother Tongue includes the Bogumiles and the Green Men legends from the time before the men turned to extreme patriarchal domination. One of the main speech patterns of the Slavic Mother Tongue is actually the kolo, the great round dance that invites males and females in together. However, the kolo was razed like the great stands and sacred groves of trees, while the males were conscripted into armies to kill and die for the few mighty males at the top of an inverted hierarchy that put men before Mother Nature.

Patriotism and war are tools of eradication that continue to find new ways to exterminate life, making war more vicious and war crimes more brutal. The groves and the trees that stand as mute witnesses to these atrocities represent one of the "clans of Mother Earth, source and center of the social groups. [There is] multiple divinity appearing to Paleolithic clan mothers,"[2] which is also true of the kolos of today. Although kolos exist and a few clan mothers have survived, they are precious few in number. Dancing the round kolo creates a kinetic binding memory practice that is integral to the partnership between men and women and can facilitate the healing and restoration of imbalances in the gender divide.

Bosnian male warriors often spoke to me in hushed tones of hearing wounded or dying men calling for their mothers.

Tears threatened to invade our conversations and words stopped altogether as the men reflected on this stranger-than-fiction effect of sharing their trauma. The universal memory of their mothers' kinetic binding—the act of nurturing, breastfeeding, and holding her child—takes hold in moments of extreme anguish. Many told me that they had not danced the kolo in years, and I wondered how they got any kinetic binding memories as an adult. We know that people who are either not touched or touched only in violence develop psychological disturbance as a result. How were these men supposed to heal themselves and stop the violence that was all but expected of them when all of their physical contact contained an element of violence? When they touch others, these former warriors have only the faint memory of how to do so with love or kindness, and they therefore perpetuate violence in themselves and as a ripple effect through their families and cities.

During the Balkan war in the 1990s, many refugees hid in the forests,

2 Joanna Hubbs, *ibid.*,

claiming later that the trees had saved their lives. Bosnian legends speak of the Bogumile Kings who lived in the dense forest in houses roofed in gold. Hidden for a thousand years since the slaughter of the Bogumiles by the church in Rome, these legendary houses are the subject of many happy plans and daydreams about finding the lost Bogumile treasures.

The father sky god tribes—the descendants of the Indo-Europeans, Aryans, and Kurgans—use trees in many violent forms. In the alpine mountainsides near Novi Travnik, Bosnia, whole tracts of relatively virgin forest tower over the town. Snipers fired at will during the Balkan War from the towering trees that wrap the hillsides of the land. At the same time, the only place the Bosnian refugees could hide was in the forests among the snipers. One woman explained to me how they positioned their bodies shoulder to shoulder with the snipers in a hideous parody of the kolo posture so that they were not visible through the rifle scopes trained on their town.

A Novi Travnik Muslim war survivor who was left paralyzed and in a wheelchair somehow crawled up into the surrounding, heavily treed mountain foothills and carefully detonated his stash of grenades, killing himself and destroying the landscape around him. He took his masculine, patriarchal machines of war and the feminine, living landscape with him into death. Completely dismembered just as Dionysus was, the paraplegic war survivor took his life near the time of the fall equinox, just as the world gave its last harvest and prepared for the dormant winter. His friends spoke to me of looking for new, green shoots of plant life on the very spot of his dismemberment, recalling the Green Man legends of rebirth and regeneration associated with the Bogumiles.

Working fields

Another war survivor, a paraplegic living near Novi Travnik in his own small house, received weekly visits from a close friend who fought alongside him in the Balkan War. His friend spoke of the paraplegic's deepening depression and despondency, stemming not only from his war-time actions but also the pain of living without his legs. One day, when his friend went to check up on him after not hearing from him in days, he pounded on the front door. When he pressed the doorbell, the house heaved and roared as the grenades exploded and shattered the simple small house into tiny fragments. The paraplegic still sat in his wheelchair by the front door after having killed himself and his friend, a testament to the rule of violent and unnatural law that men are pushed into living.

THE IMPACT:

Bosnian males sitting in cafés facing the their reflections in the tiny demitasse cups of steaming thick coffee face what they did in the wars and what they have not done in protecting life, limb, and home. Perhaps, as one young Bosnian male warrior claimed, he was killing off parts of himself that were Catholic, Muslim, or Orthodox. In the end, the South Slavic males eradicated the Bogumile within them, killing off their own regenerative capabilities and shattering the troika of life/death/life, leaving only a linear path to death. The loss has given the South Slavs one hundred years of war and no viable leadership from which to orchestrate a peaceful and harmonious civilization.

Bogumile Standing Stone near Novi Travnik in mountains

I have long vowed that my own son would not be forced into an army or to submit to the unnatural, patriarchal laws that would commit genocide on his true manhood, what being male really is. From my son and other brave men, I have learned the vast and compassionate character of a true male. The true man sees his place in the male/female continuum and seeks balance, not dominance. He recalls the trauma of events that have shaken this balance, and he suppresses his own desire for individual superiority in the search for a greater superiority—the superiority of a civilization that lives peacefully, a land where his sons do not have to shed blood simply to survive. A true man sees that women do not take from but rather add to his masculinity, his part in the larger humanity of the world, and he sees that a world in which women are safe is also a world in which their sons and husbands are safe.

Danica Anderson

Journal drawing of Ahmica-Vitez women war crimes survivors

CHAPTER 7

Evoking the White Birch Tree Council

WHEN AND WHERE I BORE WITNESS:

A month after September 11th, 2001, I continued my Kolo Trauma work with the Novi Travnik Kolo Sumejja women despite the hatred swirling in the aftermath of the destruction of the Twin Towers in New York City by an all-male group of terrorists. The town of Ahmica, site of the massacre of 150 Muslims during a morning call to prayer during the Balkan Wars, is about two kilometers away from Novi Travnik. The majority of the few survivors are grandmothers who were tending the cows in nearby fields and were forced simply to watch the slaughter of their families, unable to help.

The International Criminal Tribunal for the former Yugoslavia was established to try each individual accused of war crimes or crimes against humanity. Reading the transcript of the Ahmica/Vitez war crimes trial is itself a trial. Facing the Muslim women war crimes survivors takes courage and bravery. Hearing and witnessing their stories seemed impossible, as I had to keep my hands in my pockets and not over my ears.

STORIED INSTRUCTIONS:

At first, I thought the Bosnian women from Ahmica looked like thick, walking birch trees. Their pristine white headscarves over dark dresses with creases resembled the bark of Bosnian birches. There was a hushed silence, and I felt the need to bow to them as they filed into the elementary school classroom in Novi Travnik where I was holding the February 2001 training session.

I stood back to watch the Ahmica women make a flowing entrance, just like the reverence I would give to a great stand of trees or a sacred grove.

The only times I have ever felt this crackle of lighting within me before have been in moments of raw, unadulterated beauty that I have found in my hikes and walks in nature, especially the thick, green forests of Bosnia. I heard the soft whispers of the birds, gurgling mountain streams, and the wind whistling in the boughs of the trees as the Ahmica women walked into the hall, their long dresses and head scarves rustling.

To witness and to hear the whispers of Mother Nature from these Ahmica women—more melodious than the bugles and military parades of dead, patriarchal ceremonies—is to live and breathe female sovereignty. I was experiencing my first female evocation of the White Birch Tree Council.

The Ahmica women created a great hall in the run down elementary classroom. It had no central heating and few comforts. The Ahmica women walked to a long bench that stretched along an expanse of the kindergarten schoolroom wall, and the Kolo Sumejja women and I sat in a half circle before them.

I realized that the bench was indeed a royal Mother Earth throne, and these thick white birch trees evoked a council. The Ahmica women, draped in white babushkas, signified the return to a female legal justice system. They embodied the "Old Europe"[1] Goddesses of Rejuvenation's power to redress patriarchal imbalance.

I knew that the words spoken by Ahmica women could shatter every illusion and denial I had left. But I wanted to hear every note that was going to be sung. It was as if the chant were indeed a spell that birthed the roots of sacred groves.

I leaned forward as we sat in the kolo, tuned in to their presence. One elder grandmother spoke of having no malice or hatred toward the Croatians who committed the murder of 150 Muslims during an early morning call to prayer. She had a resounding voice that boomed as she told story after story of dead grandchildren, daughters, sons, and husbands.

Do white birch trees cry and wail? One of the Ahmica grandmothers imparted the richest notes to the White Birch Tree Council. We learned that she had been unable to speak since the loss of five members of her family one morning not so long ago. Yet without man-made words, she could utter the notes of that grief so clearly that all of us in the kolo circle were sobbing.

We all grew paler and paler as we heard the verdicts from the White Birch Tree Council. The patriarchs had ensilaged extinction, annihilating the trees in the forest, and the tree-women of Ahmica, and their sisters across the globe. They demanded retribution, speaking as the very Goddesses of Rejuvenation.

Each of the women iconized the Bird Goddess, the Snake Goddess, and Baba Yaga, the archetypal leaders of a long-past matrifocal civilization. We have found clay artifacts of this peaceful society dating from the 5th millennium BCE. Resurrected in the White Birch Tree council, its presence was palpable in the battered school room.

The White Birch Tree Council invoked the past to redress the wrongs of the present. Their ancient grandmothers spoke through them. The ancient civilization of the South Slavic people was clearly audible as the Ahmica women canted the atrocities visited upon them.

It was almost unbearable to listen to such notes of sorrow, pain, and grief.

The grief clutched at the heart and soul. I wanted to run, but I found myself rooted to the very same spot where I stood as they cried their songs.

War crimes were ruthlessly stamped and pounded right into their very homes. It is because the home and the womb are complementary symbols that homes are bombed before office buildings. To bomb the home is to destroy the family's place of nurturing, and it carries with it the same message as rape or infanticide. It strikes at the deep core of what makes us human.

The council showed us that it will happen to all of us sooner or later, and that it was happening to us now.

In April, 2002, for my Peaceful Dimensions Conference hosted by the Sumejja kolo in Novi Travnik, Bosnia, another White Birch Tree Council of Ahmica women emerged. About fifty of us filled the home of one of the council members. Cushions patterned in traditional Bosnian and Slavic designs lined every part of the living room and kitchen. I watched these very same white birch trees flow into the room and sit cross-legged on the floor.

Dressed in their Islamic attire and full pantaloons, the Ahmica women sounded like a rushing stream of silk as they settled into their sitting position. I never have witnessed such beauty and love. I tasted the salt of my tears behind my eyes—the insight that comes of facing genocide. The love appeared from nowhere and flowed into every cell of my body.

Something powerful was happening in that moment as they sang their first person stories. I knew that Mother Earth heard their earthly cries and was called into the presence of the White Birch Tree Council. The women spoke of the overturned verdict in the beginning of 2002 by the Yugoslav War Crimes Tribunal in The Hague, The Netherlands.

The International Criminal Tribunal for the Former Yugoslavia, already reeling under massive legal and administrative misconduct, was cunning enough to hand down a decision soon after the September 11, 2001, attack in America, knowing that there would be scant attention paid because the survivors of the Ahmica massacre were mostly women and children. The reality is that most humanitarian aid agencies, including the United Nations and governmental agencies like the International Criminal Tribunal for the Former Yugoslavia, are a lethally united brotherhood.

The rule of law is a fully male rule of law. Rarely do leaders pay attention to the catastrophic effects of verdicts that fail to consider the underlying problem of cyclical violence.

Kolo Sumejja women meet with Ahmica-Vitez women war crimes survivors

Overwhelming evidence shows that over 95% of all perpetrators of violence are male, and the victims are overwhelmingly female or children. These statistics represent "normal" life for females. Most of the Bosnian women in the kolo trauma program declare that this work is neither political nor feminist, and certainly there is no mention of the "G" words: Goddess or gender.

The Ahmica women evoking the White Birch Tree Council pave the way for a great symphony, a wide range of notes as their singing voices seed a virginal forest, a sacred grove free of masculine dogma and left-brain, linear rule. I intuitively knew that the Ahmica women in this isolated village, living across the road from Croatian aggressors, experienced feminine solidarity. They not only banded together spiritually and emotionally, but even their bodies began to synchronize, including their menstrual cycles.

Nemana, a grandmother whose house was burned down since it had the unfortunate position of being next to the destroyed mosque. She stated that the intimacy and the daily rhythm of the women's acts within the lunar calendar of their menses can heal rifts between them. Since, the daily rhythm of women's acts to menses perform the same actions and share a physical bond, Nemana translated how those acts are the restoration of emotional bonds.

But she went on to observe that the intimacy is not found in being terrorized, the abject fear and violence when women are forced to hide together simply to survive violence and trauma. Terror and fear does not heal, rather, it tears the fabric of the world apart.

THE IMPACT:

The earth is filled with women who do not understand their female humanity and, instead, "become the males they worship and marry."[1] When the masculine view is privileged continually, women lose sight of the power within themselves. Surviving the violence mothers are not allowed to raise their sons to not be "men" in the way that their violent fathers and role models are "men".

Amnesia, the numbing from terror and fear has women forgetting what it means to be a woman, and more than this, to be a woman in a powerful group of women. Women, unaware of their female power and innate divinity, ends up colluding and being complicit with men with the violence via the amnesia.

Yet, it is at this very moment of being aware of collusion, the place where humanity ends is the space and place to heal.

Isn't this solidarity the interlacing roots found in a thick forest? Is it not what holds us together, what keeps the last traces of life to rejuvenate us after violence? I felt that women, especially the war crimes survivors I met in Bosnia, have gone into seclusion. Just as women once were excluded from the community during their menstrual cycles, these victims and survivors of violence are set apart by a catastrophic blood cycle born from the war crimes they have lived through.

But this cloistering has instigated the sharing of grief and the multiplying of inner divinity, moving from woman to woman as if each has lit a candle from the other's flame, creating a brighter and brighter light that could cast out the darkness of death. I felt the divinity in these two White Birch Tree Council sessions and Kolos bringing back the Slavic Great Moist Mother Earth, whose knowledge is in each strand of DNA in these women's bodies. What we must remember is that they have also passed it on to their sons; the Great Mother lives in them somewhere, too.

I often wonder whether women will one day have sovereignty or female solidarity without catastrophic menses, without gossip, without competition among women that results from living without. I wonder whether we can overcome the horizontal violence that is women's inhumanity to women and take each other's side, peacefully facing down male aggression together with compassion and love. But, love and compassion means holding those accountable even if they are their fathers, uncles, brothers, husbands and sons.

I know my inhumanity towards women in the situation of the Ahmica women. I sat comfortably in my home, watching the news like someone rubbernecking during a traffic accident, almost gleeful as I said, "How awful," as if that were helping. At one point, I realized that I had to face accountability for being so divorced and separated from my sisters' reality. As Jim Wallis says, "Benefitting from oppression means to be responsible for it."

If I can watch their suffering as if it is entertainment, then I am in the wrong. Endemic violence demands action, and I did not want to be the hapless, helpless female victim I saw either on the television screen or on my couch watching the news unfold. When I returned to Bosnia in September of 2000, I faced the women's questions: "Where were you?"

Erin Hilleary. Image of Vinca period artifact

Is it because I as a woman have not experienced female social justice and female solidarity?

If we band together, will that small group spark a tiny flame and will another group see it and pass it on? If women say a resounding "No" to the male-dominated world, will it eventually be forced to take notice? Will the young women in relatively safe countries like America learn to respect the freedom and safety they have and work to make it the reality of all girls and women around the world? Women are the majority of the world's population. Is it even possible for the men to ignore us if each of our tiny flames joins to become one purifying blaze?

Erin Hilleary

CHAPTER 8

Fish Goddess and Whirlpools & Spirals

WHEN AND WHERE I BORE WITNESS:

We usually see our reflections in mirrors, but my various trips to Novi Travnik suggest the notion that we can also see our reflections in nature. On these trips, I saw the ways in which Mother Nature reflects human behavior, showing us by her physical changes what we are doing to ourselves spiritually and emotionally as we battle on her land and spill our blood into her soil. In the area surrounding Mount Vlasic, I saw great beauty and great destruction; I saw rushing waters and dying bees.

STORIED INSTRUCTIONS:

In 2000, the Novi Travnik Mountaineers Adam and Almir showed me the Angel Caves near

Novi Travnik, Bosnia. Their entrance is marked by a wide road of stones that was once a huge riverbed. In 1937, the river disappeared overnight. The local people knew this to be a message of coming wars and the Slavic reference - Moist Mother Earth's angst. I, however, having witnessed so much, do not think Moist Mother Earth punishes, but I do believe that she redresses imbalances or places perfect tension between polar opposites.

After three raging wars on Balkan soil, the people have been forced to return to the Megalithic South Slavic way of life since so many of the modern conveniences they once relied on have been destroyed. They work in the fields, prepare the same food, and practice the same domestic arts that their ancestors engaged in thousands of years ago. These small acts are reenacted and woven into the fabric of their present moments because so much is unavailable to them in the aftermath of war. The return to the Megalithic South Slavic way of life provides something new, however.

It heals *uvreda*, the wound on the Bosnian spiritual landscape where one million landmines remain hidden. The water in the Angel Caves may have disappeared overnight, just as the Bosnian way of life did, but the Bosnian people have traversed the troika of life/death/life and lead something of a postmortem existence. They see that which was once lost to them but their oral memory traditions, epigenetic process is in the DNA codes that transmit their intergenerational wisdom.

They see visions of the South Slavic Fish Goddess artifacts among the eddies, spirals, and whirlpools of water crisscrossing Bosnia, emerging from death into an existence that is richer than anyone thought possible.

The economic collapse of post-war Bosnia affects more Muslims than Croatians. Croats, whose connections with the West and the Catholic Church often have funding to ease the financial disaster besetting the former Yugoslavs. Living in the aftermath of yet another war, according to many Bosnians, is more hellish than war itself.

Women are the hardest hit and most affected by economic disaster. Searching for work and money makes many men desperate enough to become Mostar Bridge Death Divers, leaping off the bridge at dizzyingly high altitude to the river below. But women with small children clinging to their skirts do not have even this choice. Tourism explodes at the bridge paying the death divers for each leap off the bridge.

Now that the world's attention has moved on to the new, more thrilling news stories that fill our television screens, the Mostar Death Leaping divers, the real living Fish Gods and Goddesses, are just a side attraction, just like a has-been celebrity who once topped the A List. Without fresh bullets, grenades, or firebombing of the people's landscape and the people, the media has moved on, and with it, much needed foreign aid.

In 1999, I traveled to Banja Luka in the Republic of Srpksa to see my surviving relatives. On this trip, I experienced the fear of being put in the danger that surrounded my Serbian relatives every day. Careening through the mountains and the road to Banja Luka, Medex Mine Awareness staffers, Almir and Adam, drove me to a center in the middle of town. Almir and Adam were visibly cautious and tense, driving through what was Bosnia before the war but was now called the Republic of Serbia.

They covered the Medex Mine Awareness sign on their tiny, battered car, and Almir, the driver, told jokes in an effort to lighten the situation. He wondered how on earth he, a Muslim, had come to be driving a Serb/American to see her Serb relatives in a town that had once been part of his country.

I greeted my first cousin Branko's widow, who looked older but still the same. She dismissed Almir and Adam in an abrupt fashion. I felt my first inkling of fear and insecurity, where I had thought to find welcome and comfort. She preferred to walk to being in the car with the young Muslims. I was given strict instructions not to speak Serbian aloud, since she feared that I would reveal my American accent. Her nails, biting into my arm through my thick coat, felt like hundreds of stinging bees.

Though I knew that her hatred was born of pain and fear, I shivered nonetheless.

Since her home had no central heating, I ended up sleeping on the couch near the stove after one night. During my stay, I went to look at my cousin Branko's art work. Branko was an architect with strong artistic instincts. His father, married to my father's twin sister, was a well-known wood-carving artisan whose work appears in many of the former Yugoslavia's cultural museums. It was hard to imagine Branko in a soldier's uniform. He was a sensitive artist with many intellectual friends from various ethnic groups.

Branko's widow described his emotional turmoil because he did not want to fight or be in the army. He feared that he would recognize his Muslim friends in the enemy he was ordered to kill. Branko's memories of his friends were ingrained, just as bees remember and return to specific flowers for pollen. Branko's widow told me bitterly that his reluctance to fight determined his death because he was sent to the front lines as an example to other soldiers who refused to fire on the enemy, whom they knew were neighbors and friends. She shared with me that she had been directed by a Serbian army official to drive to a specific location to pick up the bag of his remains.

Looking at me with pure hatred, she spat out a question: "How could you work with Muslims from Mount Vlasic where your cousin was blown up?"

I pulled out a picture of my son and gave it to her. I told her of my trip to visit the Srebrenica war crimes widows where one widow impacted me greatly. When the Srebrenica war crimes widow and I compared photographs of our sons, we saw that they were the same age and could almost have been twins. We could not tell which was Serb and which was Muslim, only that both were our sons.

I begged Branko's widow to show me how she could tell these young men apart, whether there was some school that instructs such hateful techniques.

She snapped back, "You are exactly like Branko." and reminded me that all that was left of him was twenty pounds of remains in a nondescript bag. While she had to be able to tell "friends" from "enemies" in order to survive every day, I could see from my American vantage point that there really were no differences. Which of us was right?

The South Slavic love of the earth appears in their agricultural practices and animal husbandry. Bee-keeping is still a significant source of nourishment and income in Bosnia, and their bee-keeping practices still contain Paleolithic and Neolithic bio-culinary memories. Since what they do and how they live within the environment is paramount, the Slavs are guardians of eternal memory, but these memories need to be refreshed to be stored for use by future generations.

Yagoda Sestic supports herself with selling paintings – Banja Luka, Serbia

We know that formerly "modern" Bosnians who had never held a shovel had to return to ancient ways of life in order to survive the war, and this occurred because they had intergenerational wisdom encoded in their DNA, showing them almost instinctively how to stay alive.

The bees' daily foraging is a kolo dance for pollen, made up of flights to flowers and blooming crops. The Slavs observing the tiny bee understand how important the bee's pattern recognition skills are in daily activities that essentially are encoded in DNA shaping our environment.

Muslim grave yard

If the bee, which has no long-term memory, lost the ability to recognize the patterns of flowers and blooms, it would die. And we would die.

The Slavs understand this as a dual predicament that can either end or perpetuate life; if we continue to dance the kolo, to pollinate, to *live,* then we refresh the patterns that we will pass on to our children so that they, too, will survive. What we are talking about are the oral memory traditions, a science of rituals utilizing the epigenetic process. Diverse cultures, and indigenous practices understand culture has its roots in biology.

Surviving the war and its aftermath means that empty pantries, kitchens without microwaves, and the lack of money to buy anything, even if there were well-stocked shelves in the stores, become paths leading to a subtle, intuitive shift into ancient Slavic consciousness. For the past decade, after my trauma treatment and training in Novi Travnik, two brothers would tuck glass jars of their honey into my luggage as I left. The memories of pre-war life and all that they have lost are expunged by the brothers' ability to produce a glass jar of honey. What the brothers remember are the bees, the honey, and the flowers, not the catastrophe of war and its aftermath.

The brothers told me that the bees were dying out, and that *grabancijas,* or vampires, were the culprits. The *grabancijas* represent a malevolent, wandering spirit who is forced to attend thirteen schools of female wisdom (including migration, wisdom, and memory) before being allowed to enter the *Vrzino Kolo. Grabancijas* is blind with money and ego, and he meets death through a series of labors that take place in a forest near bodies of water with a dead woman and the divine Goddess, Moist Mother Earth.

The *Grabancijas* are taught by the witches, the Slavic Bird Goddess, and Mother Nature to dance the *Vrzino kolo* only after attending the thirteen schools of the Kolo, or feminine wisdom. The depraved masculine is forced to encounter the feminine aspects before he can attain a higher state. He must participate in the Kolo, to dance the circle that connects us all. Eventually, the man can perform a dialogue with all sentient beings, both animals and people, when he is able to manifest his true spirit, which he has learned to do from the Great Mother.

The brothers said that the genocide during the Balkan Wars parallels the demise of the bees, because we do not know the true culprits, or even whether they are physical or spiritual. We see a reflection of our own inhumanity reflected in the deaths of creatures that nourish us and have provided income for survivors of the war and the subsequent economic collapse.

The death of the bees, like the disappearance of the water in the Angel Caves, is a message from Mother Earth. She shows us a reflection of ourselves to remind us of what we have become, but the subtext of this message is a reminder of what we once were: peaceful, matrifocal, Goddess-worshippers in tune with nature. Through thousands of years of observation, recorded in their round dances, songs, chants and daily lives, South Slavs instinctively understood how to preserve a library with records beyond books, hard drives right inside the brain, DNA, and body.

When the Slavic people returned to their ancestral lands and lives after the war, they found in mere survival, a way to thrive. They began to live the sacred, elevating mundane acts to the extraordinary. What we would consider beneath us or tedious small acts are now direct, sacred encounters showing how our brains have evolved to take in visual experiences and repetitive somatic movements, from churning butter to choosing healing herbs, and encoding them for human survival.

Both the bees' foraging for pollen and daily domestic chores are sacred, according to South Slavic grandmothers. Just as pollination perpetuates the life/death/life cycle, the tasks of the *domovi,* the home, are sacred reminders of the continuity of life beyond individual lives. We use the idiom "busy as a bee" to describe a hard worker, but to South Slavic women, this is a recognition of the importance of their household work, their nurturing labors performed in the *domovi,* at once the immediate family dwelling and the temple of the ancestors whose wisdom still contributes to daily life.

THE IMPACT:

Suddenly, I felt the chill of the announcement from Fatima, Kolo Sumejja's eldest member. After the release of three Croatian war criminals by the International Criminal Tribunal for the Former Yugoslavia, Fatima explained the verdict basically reads as Muslims to killing Muslims.

Because no verdict was handed down and the criminals were simply freed, many Muslims felt unable to live in a world that would allow this. It was as if *grabancijas* wandered throughout the wars, depraved without the instructions of the thirteen schools of the Kolo; it seemed that the Male, the aggressor, would never face punishment.

The Mostar death leaps, free cigarettes, alcohol, all reflect the turning inward of hatred. Now we are practiced at killing ourselves across the globe. I think of the environmental disasters, the constant wars throughout the globe at any given time, the hunger, the rapes, and the fact that the very water we drink is polluted with toxic chemicals from products that we continue to purchase.

Novi Travnik, Bosnia- Herzegovina- Land Mine Sign behind the home

What better masons to emulate than the bees?

The ancient remains of a *domovi* in Butmir, outside of Sarajevo, Bosnia, and numerous ancient *pechs,* ovens that resemble beehives, commemorate the bees as the original South Slavic masons. Beehive ovens exist and are used to this day in South Slavic regions. The patterns in the kolos that we dance are hauntingly similar to the bee's flight paths as they pollinate the blooms in the meadows. But do they not also reflect the haunting pattern of genocide and death in my own family in the former Yugoslavia?

My healing trauma work with Muslims divided me from my family, who could not countenance my work with their "enemy." My cousin Branko died because of his commitment to peace and his refusal to kill those who might have been friends and certainly could not be so different from him. My son, the near twin of the son of a Srebrenica war widow, would have been in Branko's position had he lived in Bosnia during the war. Both are merely in different places within the troika of life/death/life?

The South Slavic brothers and their Mt. Vlasic beehives reflect our whole species, held by a fragile thread such as the tiny bee or the photographs of two sons who looked exactly alike. According to the Slavs, there are thirteen kolo schools of instruction that help us memorialize the dead and their life experiences, encoding them for future generations as we become living libraries.

Supposedly, an insect does not have a large enough brain to recognize faces. Perhaps it is more a matter of being more than the sum of its parts according to Slavs. In a study (2005) by Adrian G. Dyer[1], the lead researcher reported how bees can learn to recognize human faces in photographs and remember them for two days. Dryer stated that, "if bees can learn to recognize humans in photos, then they reasonably might also be able to recognize real-life faces. On the other hand, he remarked, this probably isn't the explanation for an adage popular

1 World Science, December 9, 2005- also appearing in Journal of Biological Experiments

in some parts of the world—"that you shouldn't kill a bee because its nest mates will remember and come after you."

That's the marvel I have for the South Slavic grandmothers of the ancient past simply understood the bee's constant flitting between the most aromatic flowers as a conceptual language of thought. A language distinct from language itself and that communicates the ultimate cycle, the universal Kolo, the understanding that we are all interconnected.

Knowing that my cousin died upon the breast of Mt. Vlasic, the blind grabancijas are still creating their destruction in the aftermath of war. What I learned is that I have insight so painful it only serves to inform me that I am alive and my cousin is not, along with the Srebrenica widow's son. I ask what's the difference?

Connie Simpson
Image based on
Bird Goddess artifacts

CHAPTER 9

Book of Veles

When and where I bore witness. From March 1999 to the present day, I have worked with a tiny fraction of the over three million refugees in the former Yugoslavia[1], in Ahmica-Vitez and Novi Travnik, Bosnia. It was October 2001, a mere two weeks after the World Trade Towers were sent to the underworld in a horrific attack on innocents.

In Bosnia, most of the women and children set the stage for evolutionary approaches, since these women and children are the invisible and the most vulnerable. The women's evolutionary approaches surmounting what most would say are impassable obstacles and arduous struggles are largely ignored by those humanitarian and justice agencies that were there to help. There was little funding—if any—for the invisible and the most vulnerable. In the end, these women had no choice but to move forward and evolve.

STORIED INSTRUCTIONS

The Book of Veles, describing the origins of the Slavic, Baltic, Serbian, and Polish tribes is hotly debated, with many in academic fields refuting its authenticity. Written on planks of wood, the Book of Veles' sacred data is a Slavic phenomenon that anchors an integrated transcendence of its peoples. Beneath all of the arguments against the Book of Veles' existence is a powerful Slavic technology triggering radical shifts of consciousness and healing practices that recover a coherence of harmony.

I know the mass forced march from South Slavic homes of three million people during the Balkan War is not a migration. Nor would a forced march be chronicled in the Book of Veles. The forced march of the South Slavs is a formidable shadow over their way of life for integrated transcendence concerning their oral tradition literature practices. Given the South Slavs' relations with the Moist Mother Earth, the Book of Veles is a geocentric map of land and seascapes vital to the South Slavs since it represents their migration to a land of Blood and Honey. The blood is not the spilt blood of wars or genocide but the rivers, the waters that feed the land into honey: abundance. Like the Book of Veles, the land of blood and honey is an open-ended evolution borne from the ashes.

Contrary to what we might expect, increasing the ties to their Slavic Moist Mother Earth is shown through the milk from the Ahmica-Vitez grandmother's cows and the eggs from her chickens that feed the remaining Ahmica-Vitez war crimes survivors' family members. And it was the increased communion with their cows and planting in the fields that had the Ahmica-Vitez grandmother out of the house on the early morning of April 15, 1993, when the slaughter of her family was perpetrated. According to the Ahmica-Vitez women war crimes survivors, their land, grassy meadows, and crops attracted genocide, not the god of Veles.

1 Julie A. Mertus, *"War's Offensive on Women," The Humanitarian Challenge in Bosnia, Kosovo and Afghanistan,"* Kumarian Press, 2000)

'Now they have the Muslims killing

What is interesting is the Slavic and Baltic customs preserved in the Book of Veles, particularly the story of the Russian father named Bogumir and mother, Slavuni, who owned a great deal of livestock and whose children married across the tribes. Bogumir and Slavuni's children represent the Slavic, Baltic, and Polish tribes as one family, a harmony with replenishing healing balance achieved. Despite the Goths' and Huns' terrible warfare at that time, the outcome produced peoples protecting and preserving the wisdom of the Moist Mother Earth.

Traces of the guardianship and preservation are found in the still practiced rituals among the Slavs. One of many Slavic female cultural practices is to feed snakes milk so that the gardens flourish and protect the *domovi*. For Baltic peoples, Velines, a Lithuanian equinox (around April), is full of feast celebrations for the dead, portraying the ancient links to the Dionysus and Bacchus rituals.

Fascinatingly, the Spring equinox would have the Bird migrations coinciding with the feast in reverence to the Bird and Snake Goddess. But, for the Ahmica-Vitez women war crimes survivors, April and the spring equinox now heralds mass murder. What is chilling is how the archaeomythology has the god Veles attracted to the open meadows, the same type of landscape in the village of Ahmica-Vitez.

The Ahmica-Vitez war crimes survivors were bitter and hostile toward the Yugoslav War Crimes Tribunal for a few years after 2001. However, what was strangely absent was hatred, despite how deeply the Ahmica-Vitez mothers and grandmothers distrusted the criminal court and all humanitarian institutions and justice systems.

The tribunal adjudicated and upon testimony released the Croat war crimes criminals. If we look at the word origin of testimony comes from the Latin 'testis' and testament where grabbing onto your testicles meant the truth. The migration toward justice was rendered invisible after a Muslim not from the Ahmica-Vitez village or around at the time of the slaughter of one hundred and fifty Muslims on April 15, 1993, testified that the three Croatian war criminals were not the ones who committed the massacre. His testimony made a mockery of the proceedings that were designed to bring justice and only set the cause back further, adding new reasons to hate and distrust.

I did not know how to express the reality that it is our sons, fathers, brothers, uncles, and grandfathers who, along with women, have allowed the massacres generation after generation. I did not speak of this to the Ahmica-Vitez women war crimes survivors. Fatima, an elder in Novi Travnik's Kolo Sumejja, remarked after the release of the three Croatian war crimes criminals, which was shortly after September 11, 2001, "Now they have the Muslims killing themselves; no one else did it." Her anger was clear, as was her acceptance of life in the aftermath of war with no expectation of justice. Fatima channeled anger into healing and harmony, not hatred.

Nemana and her neighbor arrived early in summer of 2005 to announce their desire to tell the story of a profound woman who once lived in Ahmica-Vitez. During the war, she fled from her home where she was known to have great passion and love for her rich array of flowers and thriving vegetable patch.

themselves; no one else did it."

After the war, she trudged home back to Ahmica-Vitez. The small community had nothing, but this woman shared all she had. It became obvious that cancer had eaten through her body, but she was joyous to be home and living on the land again.

She was the main force in the Ahmica-Vitez war crimes survivorship toward thriving without hate. I was told that she found joy where most found war crimes, hardship, and lack. So infectious was her loving life and Ahmica-Vitez that Nemana and her neighbor remembered her vividly enough to replace their horrific memories of the faces of the dead and dying with this woman's smiling face.

Taking the note pad from my lap while I sat in Nemana's kitchen, I agreed with the women who told me that it was time to write this woman's story to share with others who could know her at least through our words. Stunned by their tutelage, I immediately thanked them. I took the notepad back and told them she would be in my personal Book of Veles. I did not want her erased from the pages meant for the educated.

Julie Mertus wrote "The Suitcase Refugees," and her study also outlines the invisible and most vulnerable targets, such as the daughters, mothers, and grandmothers. Mertus' research estimates that 75% of global refugees are women and children, carrying little more than a single suitcase at best. The middle-aged and elderly women remained well below one percent in terms of receiving any funding for aid. There is no line item in any humanitarian aid agency that was or is secured for the middle-aged and elderly women or titled "small acts."

When I met with the Sarajevo Human Rights general undersecretary Zivica Abadic, now retired, she stated that illiteracy (with over thirty percent females described as illiterate) was rising in the aftermath of the 1990s Balkan war and that unreported domestic labors mostly done by middle-aged and elderly women do not have pensions and are at slave labor rate of pay, if there were a salary. [2]

Chain smoking and thin, short hair dyed black, Zivica Abadic spoke of the Bosnian South Slavic fathers living under an unemployment rate soaring past 80% in the aftermath of war twelve years later, who now refuse to pay school fees for their daughters. The range of education among the women is staggeringly poor.

THE IMPACT

To the invisible and most vulnerable, the packing up of their hand ground coffee and baked sweets to take to the meetings with both the Ahmica-Vitez and Srebrenica war crimes survivors was nothing more to them than simply sharing coffee and baklava, something they do at home as much as they can. In fact, drinking the small demitasse cups of thick Bosnian coffee numerous times during the day allowed the sharing of their blood and honey first person stories.

What is deceptive about their hand-wrapped packages of cakes and savory cheese pita packed in worn suitcases is that the Novi Travnik women war survivors are privy to war crimes stories not even whispered in any tribunal courts or international courts. The invisible and most

2 July , 2005 meeting Sarajevo Helsinki Human Rights Office with the general undersecretary and Kolo Sumejja Novi Travnik, Bosnia

vulnerable are the ones who are bearing witness and serving female justice to the most terribly wounded and traumatized women and children.

But what took place are the first person stories, their primary healing tools for trauma and the real Book of Veles—the real blood and honey stories. What I learned from these women is that what lives on long after we die are these narratives, the Book of Veles. The Book of Veles and Bogumiles do not reside only in the former Yugoslav region, but also in Bulgaria. Bulgarian guardianship of the Book of Veles was maintained by the Pavlikeni, Bulgarian heretics. The Bogomils (also Bogumiles) were a sect dating from 950 AD through the Middle Ages, which coincides with the Book of Veles dates.

But the Book of Veles was not just known to the Balkan peoples and tribes. A Cyprian monastery is referred to as being pure Bogumile. The Catholic Church in Rome hailed the Cyprian monastery as being promiscuous in its beliefs and practices. The church's criticism most likely refers to the inclusion of the divine feminine and the Lost Goddesses: Balkan Bird and Snake Goddesses of Regeneration. Mostly, targeted and attacked by the educated clergy, the Book of Veles heightened hatred for the female narratives of their life experiences and capacity to heal their families and communities. It's all in the twist of gender, that of male gender in the Book of Veles.

South Slavic female justice is an evolutionary process that occurs through small acts done consistently and with great love. Sweeping up after the wars and baking sweets while boiling thick coffee in a wide-based and narrow-necked pot called a *jesva* has been done silently for generations, behind the scenes of what was cited as momentous humanitarian aid and policies that did not support or recognize them.

But the kolo trauma format is performed by mostly illiterate, invisible females who are known to experience the most damage. The educated and humanitarian aid agencies know this and still do nothing. Of course, they are invisible to you and me as we ask, "How did this happen without the media making sure that we all knew about it?"

Promiscuous in their healing tutelage, the Kolo Sumejja with the Kolo trauma format worked and played with those most targeted by educated humanitarian and ruling entities, which saw them as luscious victims justifying large grants of funding for their pockets. Despite the lack of funding and their illiterate, invisible status, the women swung through Bosnia using their para-professional trauma skills with the Ahmica-Vitez women and the Srebrenica women who lost thousands of their male relatives in one day.

No humanitarian policy or justice system has a written procedure or a budget line for bakery items and thick Bosnian coffee specifically for the invisible and the most vulnerable targets. The grandmothers, the elderly women, are erased and ignored, not just in Bosnia's humanitarian crisis but globally. Not a single grandmother, elderly widow, or the infirm who are the invisible and most vulnerable sit on councils, governing policy, and decision concerns. Nor are they asked for their wise input or to express the reality and truth of their experiences by their courts and humanitarian agencies. It does not matter. The women have their Book of Veles and now this chapter is for the educated who have not seen them until now.

Erin Hilleary

CHAPTER 10

The Kolo

WHEN AND WHERE I BORE WITNESS

From the moment I stepped back into Bosnia, landing in the old Sarajevo airport in March of 1999, I have witnessed the preserved remains of the kolo, the traditional folk round dance. I have watched dancers in the circle, wholly unaware of the practical application of the dance to healing the collective South Slavic community.

STORIED INSTRUCTIONS

One of the most beautiful towns in Bosnia is Travnik. Its mosque's minaret is on the left side because of the beautiful, rushing mountain waters nearby. The mosque is decorated with a girding of trees as if to remind future generations of the need to nurture life; here, we see a pattern for avoiding domestic violence as we are reminded to nurture women as we would trees. The imam school is a short distance away, right across the street from Blue Waters Café, where Austro-Hapsburg Archduke Ferdinand drank coffee hundreds of years ago. Travnik is the mother city to Novi Travnik, and during the war, this city was refuge for thousands, especially for rape camp victims.

Travnik has beauty that grabs your breath and barely relinquishes a draught of thin, mountain air in return. As a result, you are held breathless when surrendering to the landscape. Like that of the countryside near Travnik, female geography is mapped with its spherical mountains and undulating hillsides. The very land evokes substantive meanings from the past and imports it into your present moments as you circle the blue waters cascading down from the Bogumile Castle and through the twisting and winding streets with their tilting, precarious sidewalks. Beneath the streets and homes in Travnik, one can almost hear the rushing waters flowing in unknown arteries and caverns to secret destinations elevating the mysteries to rising flood stages.

The unchecked domestic violence prevalent in Travnik is known as a cultural male entitlement that is blamed, for a myriad reasons, on the women and children who are its victims. Travnik, so feminine in its spectacular geophysical beauty, is also known as the birthplace of the Bosnian winner of the 1961 Nobel Prize, Ivo Andric. Born a Croat to a strict Catholic mother, Andric proclaimed himself Serbian, perhaps in rebellion against his mother and aunt. Andric studied the Muslim, *dhimmi,* conditions that were formulated in the seventh and eight centuries by Muslim jurists and theologians and imposed on indigenous Bosnian Christians refusing Islam in the subsequent centuries.

Andric's 1945 book *The Bridge on the River Drina* focuses on the Mehmed-Pasha Sokolovich Bridge, where a massacre of Bosnians would take place nearly fifty years after his book was published. Andric's descriptions of the beauty surrounding this bridge reveal the same enthrallment in the geophysical realms in Bosnian landscapes that demands legitimacy for the kolo as well; both speak to the interconnectivity of all life. For all the beauty in his poetic description of the feminine landscapes in his books, Ivo Andric was known for beating his wife. And this did not stop him from getting a Nobel Prize and did not show him the irony of praising one aspect of feminine beauty, while destroying another.

Because of the mountainous landscape and the terrain that surrounds Travnik, war barely scraped this alluring, beautiful city. To be sure, many women spoke of the snipers who targeted them when they hung laundry out on the balcony or went to the market. Mostly, the Travnik women complained that they could not gather together and shop for food as they once did. The circle, the kolo, naturally forms when women gather together. However, many of the women talked of their heightened sense of purpose during the war, noting that even the smallest task, such as gathering firewood, took on a life-or-death aspect.

"This is not the kolo," confirmed Gjmika, a former Olympic Handball Champion for the former Yugoslavia, who resides in Travnik. Gjimika's posture is straight and athletic, and as I touched her arm to inquire about what exactly the kolo is, she turned her shoulder to me and released a tumble of gestures and words. She said it was specifically my touch on her arm. What I thought was a small gesture results in the bond that impelled me to cross the ocean to dance the kolo with her and the Kolo Sumejja women.

Again, with her startling blue eyes, she kept a flow of poetic college material pouring out of her heart, not just her mouth. When she dabbed her eyes and told me how meaningful this moment in Novi Travnik was, she shared with me the barriers of wounds and trauma that kept neighbors from helping each other to heal, from crossing the oceans that separate them, even when those distances are only a few feet.

A few kilometers away, Novi Travnik had a thriving munitions factory and a working garage for buses that crowded the town. The town lay flat, with its edges curling up and wrapping into the surrounding forests and mountainsides. Novi Travnik, however, could not be uglier in appearance.

Often, as I pass by the men sitting in cafanas and drinking a thick demitasse of coffee, I witness the shattered look of their hunched shoulders, and I wonder if they are aware of the price of the munitions manufacturing nearby. While it once employed them, it also served in the killing of so many people around

Novi Travnik, behind a central Apt. Flat, open sewers

the world in numerous wars and armed conflicts.

The men staring into their cups are alone; they have no companions, no kolo, just extreme loneliness. Any group of these men could have at its center one whose mind returns to the strafing bullets of the war. He sees not his fellow man, but soldiers and memories of the dead. The men smoke and drink their coffee as their women walk by, carrying immense packages of potatoes to plant or bags of precious flour to bake with while their children pull at their skirts. I turned to Gjmika, and she said, "No, this is not the kolo."

The grey apartment flats in both Travnik and Novi Travnik towering over the cafanas are home to many women who desire to reenact the four-thousand-year-old South Slavic Bird Goddess rituals and worship. Classically trained archeologist, Marija Gimbutas, catalogued thousands of South Slavic Bird Goddess artifacts and marveled at the peaceful Neolithic civilization that stood on the same geographic location as the former Yugoslavia.[1] I was told story after story of leaping women, both young and old, who flew out of their windows like birds whose cage doors have been left open. These women, so much like the clay artifacts

Erin Hilleary. Image based on Bird Goddess artifact

that represent the Bird Goddess, were shattered, both emotionally and physically, by the war.

The most common story I heard to explain these deaths was that the women supposedly tripped off their balconies in the aftermath of war. One daughter who lost her mother in this way murmured that, "Despite the elegance of Travnik and the sound of the roaring Blue Waters nearby, the beauty could not stop her mother's flight to the cold pavement some nine stories below."

A Novi Travnik husband whose wife plunged to her death after he left early in the morning to work, angrily reported that Bosnians call these deaths accidents when they clearly are not. I asked hesitant questions, wondering how she could have left her toddler alone so long when her husband

1 Marija Gimbutas, (1991). *The Civilization of the Goddess.* Harper CollinsSanFrancisco.

would be away at work, and why she would leave a child behind whose father still worked at a job that had not paid his salary since the war. I wondered whether she had any friends, a kolo of women to support her as she eked out an existence in a huge, grey building, pockmarked with bullet and grenade holes, where there was no central heating. I got no answers.

Novi Travnik is a few kilometers away from Travnik, but it could be worlds away. Astoundingly, right in front of a derelict police building, the healing of trauma took place in the collective community without a single political speech or inauguration. On Friday nights in Novi Travnik, when it is not a period of fasting or a holy day, such as *Ramadan,* kolo dancing is open to all. The music entrances the young and old, who join hands and dance the kolo shoulder to shoulder in the small square. The postures of the elderly and the barely toddling child are embraced lovingly and with laughter.

All this takes place in the square near what was once the police station. The police station is riddled with bullet and grenade holes, and the fragments of the shattered front window still hang from the frame. The balcony of the former police headquarters is somewhat enclosed, but it is not easy to see, since it sits behind one very old apartment building almost torn apart by mortar fire. While the sagging and bullet-ridden structure is joined to another apartment flat that held retail stores at the main level, it remains as a skull and crossbones metaphor to anyone walking by.

In 1999, the main floor of the apartment flat adjacent to the police building was nearly inaccessible because a green Volkswagen was partially melted to the cement floor of a war-ruined retail shop. It remained there for years before a new supermarket was built by what Novi Travnik citizens reported as the Mafia or black market concerns.

The reality of the Balkan War is that Novi Travnik was the front line.

Even if you were not there during the Balkan war, you would know that the police station was the frontline of the war.

The horrible irony of the police station being among the most dangerous places in the war is because, in this part of Novi Travnik, the Croats lived literally a street away from the Muslim enclave, allowing the Croat militia to fire easily out of their own homes. Many Muslim and Croat policemen died the twisted death of intergenerational hatred that leads to wars and violence, yet during the community kolo dancing, the sagging and derelict police building is on a new front line, one of life and peace, as danced by grandfathers, grandmothers, fathers, mothers, and children.

Postures are the most sacred expressions of the kolo, both the circle, and the dance. The etymology of the word "postures" reveals that its root is the word "post," which comes from a "long, upright piece of wood." This ancient root was formed from the feminine form of the Latin *ponere*, which means "to put or place." [2] Postures, as we refer to them in the kolo, describe the horizontal and vertical sacred space where the movements of the kolo offer a weaving—an embroidery if you will—with the elements. In the past decade of work in Bosnia, I have observed postures from the old, the young, and even toddlers as "depressive" and bowed by some invisible burden.

What is captivating is that the slouching posture is erased when an individual

2 John Ayto, Dictionary of Word Origins,(Arcade Publishing, New York 1990) p.406

enters the kolo round dance. I have witnessed and heard first person stories in which those who are finally heard and listened to become animated, moving into wise and loving postures and out of their bowed-down shapes. When I ask a beautiful, middle-aged Muslim woman to leave a boyfriend who has beaten her, her posture is one of denial and fear. When I listen and truly witness, she looks directly at me and positions her shoulders in alignment with mine. Her posture is erect, as if supported by the very air that surrounds us.

I advise the woman about leaving her boyfriend, suggesting that she slowly plan her release by saving money and taking clothes and other items to her daughter, who lives in another Bosnian region. As I lay out a plan of escape, she takes on an erect, vertical posture, and her arms take on a horizontal posture, as if she were a conductor leading the symphony of her new life. Her daughter called me on her mother's cell phone the very next day, crying tears of joy because someone had advised her mother to live, to embrace life. The daughter told me that she danced a kolo when her mother spoke of her weaving her plan and said that she and her mother would dance a kolo in celebration when she finally arrived.

THE IMPACT

What is friendship? Slavs and South Slavs are known for rituals and practices within their daily lives that reinforce communication with friends. Essentially, the Slavic native wisdom held within the kolo is an iconography that is danced or lived. It both symbolizes and acts out their own commemorative family practice, admitting friends into the family circle and strengthening bonds and ties. Their friends at their dining table, the picnic on the bare grass or in the fields, the threshing of their harvest, the partaking of well water carried in earthen jugs, and the churning of butter are monumentalized, re-envisioned landscapes that are collectively termed mnemnonia, which refers to a fusing of memory, a connection between memory and the physical world in which actions both release and encode memories. After a century of wars, many Bosnians do not know what defines friendship, since neighbors slaughtered neighbors, changing the meaning of the word for generations.

The world does not know friendships but encourages allies fostering global violence on a holocaustic scale unknown in Neolithic and older Ages.

This encoding was mostly passed down through women, often blind, illiterate elders, who would mnemonically access songs and poetry to encircle past, present, and future generations, describing friendship and the consequences of aligning with patriarchal, not matriarchal or matrifocal, practices.[3] The "blind Jeca" (a female singer) knew the difference between *knowing* a song and an intergenerationally implicit knowing *of* a song. The kolo dances are encoded with memory, a record of true meaning that resides between extremes—life and death, trauma and healing, friend and enemy. Since vestiges of these ancient memories are still alive today in the former Yugoslavia, will the intangible heritage of mnemonia remain a collective healing process, or is it facing eradication by overwhelming violence?

3 Holton, M., Mihailovich, V., (1997). *Songs of Serbian People: From the Collections of Vuk Karadzic.* University Press, p. 6).

Connie Simpson
Bird Goddess artifact

CHAPTER 11

The Bird Goddess

WHEN AND WHERE I BORE WITNESS

In July 15, 2005, I was facilitating another retreat in Neum, Bosnia, on the Adriatic coast, with the Kolo Sumejja women. For most of the women, a retreat would be impossible since many could not afford a bus ticket to a nearby town for less than a dollar. Being on the Bosnia Herzegovina coast allows them to retreat from their daily lives and get away from the endless drudgery of the aftermath of war. I found that as a trauma expert and therapist that this was the best possible therapy. Our leased, tattered yellow bus followed a mountainous road along the Neretva River to the Adriatic Sea.

The Kolo Sumejja women metaphorically refer to this retreat and its journey as "being given wings to fly away". The annual retreat has a trauma training and treatment component while the women are basking in the sun, placing their feet in the Adriatic waters, and being served meals. The Kolo treatment of trauma focuses on women, major caregivers, and mothers because they are the ones who sustain healing however, with one strong feature, that the women are the professors or experts and mutually exchange what they learn. Returning home, these women would heal their families and local communities.

STORIED INSTRUCTIONS

When I go to Bosnia-Herzegovina, I meet with living Bird Goddesses and Madonna Women. The glories of the past, as evidenced by Neolithic artifacts and remains, reveal the highly natural order of the world as it's essentially matrifocal assemblage. I note in the Kolo Sumejja women, the tendency to return to the matrifocal natural order in the aftermath of war.

The artifacts and ethno-anthropological remains of "Old Europe" (until 1800 BCE) are found geographically in the former Yugoslav region. The palatial ruins of *domovi* cover the landscape. These dwellings, which were used as temples and revered as resting places for ancestral spirits, are filled with clay artifacts of the Bird Goddess and Madonna. The *domovi* suggest power; not only do they loom large in the visual landscape, but they are empowering places that recall the instinctive relationship between people and Mother Earth.

Domovi iconize the ancient practices that connect us to the Moist Mother Earth, and they, therefore, pattern both mothering and nurturing for us in the modern era, revealing the importance of our spiritual inheritance. Females were revered in Neolithic Old Europe; rape and pornography were unknown. None of the archeological sites turned up any evidence of sexual trauma, or even war, for that matter. In the modern era, however, sexual trauma and war are normal fare across the globe.

The Madonna was a zoomorphic spirit, appearing in the form of a bear or bird. She was traditionally painted in red ochre to represent menstrual blood, while Black Madonna figurines attested to the ancient memory of our first mother. [1] Clay-headed figurines had neatly-incised hair that reflected the symbolic forms of the triangle; the dots were so naturalistically rendered that, despite the bird's beaked nose forms and long necks, the figurines mirrored the human face, suggesting the intertwining of the bird-spirit and the human. I realize that the same human female faces I look deeply into with the Kolo Sumejja women are living, breathing images of the Neolithic Madonna.

Nemana – Ahmica Shmica-Vittez war crimes survivor

The wingless forms of the zoomorphic Madonna found in the former Yugoslavia represent the potential to recover and consider otherwise vague mythological antiquity. The wingless forms appear to point directly to the reoccurring fables from South Slavic grandmothers that tell of giant flightless birds that lived during the age of dinosaurs. They suggest that the very wings of birds appear as the precursors to human arms and hands, presaging the more modern belief in archangels and angels.

The South Slavic Bird Goddess artifacts also maintain the iconic representation of the Widow Goddess. The Widow Goddess appears in modern accounts of Muslim genocide. July 10, 1995, the day that 8,000 to 10,000 Muslim men disappeared in front of the eyes of a Dutch "peace keeping force" into Serbian soldiers' control, is now remembered as the day of Muslim genocide. [6]

The Kolo Sumejja women from Novi Travnik and I have met with the Srebrenica widows a few times as a part of their kolo trauma outreach training. The Srebrenica women desperately hoped their male relatives were still alive as they sat at their looms weaving rugs for a living. Many of the female survivors and witnesses, Srebrenica widows of this brutality, refer to the Widow Goddess as if to ally themselves with her in their grief or to constantly resist their widow status.

The masses of widows, not just from Srebrenica, but from all over the South Slavic region, are called *Udova* or *Udovica* in Bosnian. When I arrived in Bosnia from the airport in July, 2005, I watched on television newly released videos of Serbian soldiers called Scorpions shooting thin, young Muslim men and boys in the woods.

1 Joan Marler, Ed. L. Luca Cavalli-Sforza, Genetic Evidence Supporting Marija Gimbutas' Work on the Origin of Indio-European People, (Knowledge, Ideas & Trends, Inc, Manchester, CT, 1997) p 93-101

Standing next to me as we watched, Sana Koric commented that the emotionless Scorpions must not have children, because if they did, they could not kill these young men and boys wantonly, as if for sport. I felt pains in my stomach when I replied that the Scorpions most likely were fathers, but that hatred is supreme, surpassing even humanity.

The South Slavic word *Udova* has its roots in the Indo-European terms for widow (*Vidhana*) and weaving. India's *Dhumavathi*, or *Vidhava*, equates to Bosnia's *Udova* and *Baba Yaga*. All are goddesses who represent the aspect of the Divine Mother that faces death and destruction. This kinship is identified in tracing the etymology of their names, which reveals the potentially Mesolithic origins of our universal mother tongue, which has spread and evolved over the centuries.

Tracing the universal origins of language from the original proto-Indo-European source affirms the archetypal features of the Divine Mother and discloses her migratory paths, taken so long ago as peoples spread out to new lands, taking with them an evolving language and religion. The migratory paths taken were to move toward abundance, to encounter intensified learning environments while experiencing awe and the wonders of the world.

Grandmother who begged for death

There are many stories of *Udova* in the former Yugoslav region. In a once-elegant mid-century building owned by a war survivor, a grandmother has become decayed and begun a descent into ruin, much like the building in which she lived. Entering that building, we see an elder grandmother living alone and surrounded by refugees who have brought in squalor and filthy living conditions. Her situation, however, is better than that of others. Many women live in the streets or even in ditches, begging for food and for some semblance of the life they lived before the war.

In the aftermath of the Balkan War, the grandmother's only child, a daughter, left for Canada with her own two young daughters. Suffering ill health, the grandmother pleads for death. A Roma matriarch from among the building's refugee population helps her to drink and eat, becoming the only support system for her. All other health care and elder care systems now require private funds, and her daughter in Canada could barely afford a phone call to her mother once a month. Learning a new language and finding childcare for two young children have forced the daughter into squalid conditions that ensures that she cannot come back to her mother's aid.

The grandmother quietly stated that she could die now.

Her daughter's and grandchildren's immigration to Canada was the result of a migratory urge rather than the dreaded diaspora effect. I was hard-pressed to agree with her but remained silent. Diaspora tears apart family life and is a festering wound that leads to situations like the one I witnessed, in which a grandmother dies among strangers and filth. Migration does not break family ties as diaspora does. With migration, there is the possibility of return, or at least of the family that has been left behind to join those who have moved away. Diaspora, however, is a much larger, more desperate shift in a society, taking place when many have few options. Without the time or resources to save and plan for a move, immigrants often become refugees, which can lead them to even worse conditions than those they escaped.

Grandmother with Romano mother who took over her apt and cared for her

Povreda is the Bosnian word for trauma, and it means to injure, to push down, or infringe on another. Its root word, *vreda,* translates to "worth or value." The word "wound" in Bosnian is *uvreda*, and its connection to *vreda* highlights the belief that wounds are blessings of great worth, residing in the purview of the Widow Goddess, the Slavic Baba Yaga. *Uvreda* also refers to the mortification of death. Too many widows and Madonnas who lost their children to war and endless hatred mirror the diaspora itself, reflecting the widespread destruction of their country and the horrific dislocation of people that has affected not just Europe but the entire world.

Kolo trauma treatment and training attends to and heals the socio-political changes that the diaspora has brought to South Slavic families. The kolo training, through the annual trek to the Aegean Adriatic Sea, reproduces migratory behaviors, not diaspora, and works to strengthen community, not weaken it by their constant updating of their trauma adaptive skill set.

All treks to visit other women in their local communities ripple out across former Yugoslavia, through women not men, modeling not lecturing, and their adaptive skill set. With the outreach pouring through the hands of a small kolo group, Sumejja, the journeys are but migrations not diaspora. Friends from before the war residing elsewhere would eagerly meet the bus and joyously sing out love when they come into town. I marveled at how the women Madonna, Bird Goddesses on their migrations have cleaned up after the war and refused diasporas' impact upon their families and friends.

The eldest in the Kolo Sumejja were the most rowdy Madonnas and South Slavic Bird Goddesses. The women of the Kolo Sumejja were Gjmika, a handball champion from the former Yugoslavia; Fatima, a widow who owned a restaurant in Novi Travnik before the war; Rasema, another widow who lost her sons and two husbands; and Sana Koric, leader of the Kolo Sumejja women, a family owned photography store. They all exchanged jokes and laughter throughout the night and the trip. Whenever there was laughter, tears of both joy and sadness would appear. This would occur when the women sang bar songs or folk songs that brought the whole bus to tears. It was hard to tell if the tears came from laughter or sadness.

I would toss and turn, struggling to sleep, and think of how the Kolo Trauma Treatment and Training Retreat to Neum on the Adriatic coast, represents a cyclic migration, treating trauma without uttering a single therapeutic word. In Novi Travnik, these women are effectively still prisoners of war, but the annual retreat affords them an escape from patriarchal rule; that it takes place on the coast signals a return to female territory as the feminine ocean pulls us toward her.

Removal from the traumatic aftermath of war, in which these women are imprisoned in stereotypical gender roles considered dull and punitive, requires little coercion, if any. Most of the women are only qualified for underpaid jobs and unpaid positions. Privately, I thanked the individual donors for providing funding for this trip.

When we arrived in the morning, some of the bread had hardened. Fatima offered me the choice of feeding either the fish or the birds once we arrived at our lodgings. The intelligence portrayed by Fatima and the women could not be ignored as I placed the hard bread in the embroidered cloth that bore the image of the Bird Goddess. At our lodgings, I placed the bread out on the covered patio where the birds immediately swooped down to eat.

Introducing yoga to the Kolo Sumejja women would make a dream sitcom.

The somatic heritage in the kolo eases the transitions into yoga postures for most while Fatima complains and protests against the exercise. Laughing, Fatima said all she can see is the other women's rear ends during yoga. This sent most of the middle-aged and older women into fits of laughter. However, when I slowed down or titrated, the movements and the postures, Fatima and a few other women reported that deep, internal movements occurred on their own.

One of the women stated that she felt instinctively that her shoulders and upper arms contained memory, perhaps of being able to fly. Understanding the complexity of their indigenous intelligence—their intangible heritage, if you will—my awe was profound. I asked her to teach me about it. For the rest of the hour, the Kolo Sumejja women's instructions were extraordinary, bringing authentic, deep, internal somatic movements, or what I would call Slavic thaumaturgic practices.

On our return trip, we made an unplanned stop in the mountains of Gorni Vauf, Bosnia. Since we left in the early morning, I insisted that the bus door be left open, as I did not want to swelter in the bus. My edict made most of the Kolo Sumejja women laugh and shake their heads at me.

Dead chicken cleaned by the Croat mother who lost her two sons in the Balkan War

Some of them argued that the wind on their skin would give them colds or sore muscles, and I retorted that fainting from heat exhaustion would be worse. I reminded them that birds use the wind and do not catch colds or have sore muscles.

Of course, our tattered yellow bus broke down in front of a farmhouse. An old Croatian woman—a stara Baba—was plucking a chicken that had been killed that day by a vehicle. Her husband was on the front porch, sitting on an old kitchen chair in front of a small, square table holding his beverage of choice—alcohol. At first glance, one can tell that this Baba maintains the farm, the home, and the hearth. She is dressed in all black, just like an *udova*. Her somber attire and her posture as she bent over to pluck the dead chicken represented *udova* perfectly. The compelling imagery that came to my mind is the incarnated Mother Nature—the Slavic Baba Yaga—come to life as the tiny feathers filled the air.

I meditated on the chasm separating the two scenes before me: the Slavic Baba Yaga and her chicken awaiting the oven provided a heartbreaking contrast to the sublimity of the Bosnian Mountains. As the Kolo Sumejja women and I took in this scene, this Baba spoke of watching the Srebrenica television report that I had seen when I arrived in Bosnia-Herzegovina. Her sobs made it difficult for me to understand her. The Baba moved into a standing position, as if she were preparing to speak before an audience, and said one sentence: "All mothers are the same when they lose their sons."

Stating that she had only one wish—that her husband would stop drinking—the Baba mourned the deaths of her two Croatian sons and all children lost in the melee of war and hatred that had pervaded her civilization throughout the generations. The South Slavic Widow Goddess' wisdom for Baba's *uvreda* was that her sons are our sons. I will add that all daughters are our daughters, sisters, mothers, and grandmothers.

IMPACT

South Slavic women once intuitively knew the internal rhythm of Mother Nature's calendar. After experiencing the horrors of WWI, WWII, and the Balkan War of the 1990s in their homes and wombs, they appear to have amnesia concerning their Slavic thaumaturgic practices. No longer able to advocate for the birds or themselves, South Slavic females are barely surviving the aftermath of yet another war.

Not only have they experienced the emotional disaster of catastrophic violence, but the economic crisis forced the former Yugoslavian currency, the dinar, out of existence in 1993. This led to increased inflation, poverty, and suffering, especially among the most vulnerable citizens, the women and their children. The same economic effect is being felt by European Union, Crete, Greece, Spain and the United States are slipping into the same disaster that comes from a patriarchs' economy.

But if we learn from these women, the Gift Economy, a theory originating from Genevieve Vaughan has been in practice with the South Slavic women for a century. Vaughan states "the thread of gift giving and receiving begins in every life in the unilateral need satisfaction provided by mothers."[2]

While the Kolo treatment and training, including yoga practice and performance of the traditional round dances, recalls the worship of the Balkan Bird Goddess, hostile patriarchal governments with their wars and environmental disasters call repeatedly on organized religion, which still thrives in the aftermath of war. Most of what I was able to witness being resurrected in the Slavic women of the former Yugoslavia, is a mere shell of what was once the Balkan Bird Goddess in Neolithic eras.

2 Theory of The Gift Economy http://www.gift-economy.com/theory.html

However, the fragile shell refused to break, presaging a return to Neolithic practices, as evidenced by their use of wood-burning stoves and fireplaces and their reclamation of their own sustenance, raising chickens and cows and planting gardens to feed their families. Many of the women who have returned to these practices are long-time city dwellers, completely unaccustomed to meat that does not come already cut and wrapped in paper or cellophane.

Many of them have not planted a seed except for perhaps flowers. Nor did they consider how their food gets to the fluorescent-lighted stores from which they purchased it before the war. Now though, they must return to the wisdom of their grandmothers to feed their children, and in doing so, they call up the vestiges of the Bird Goddess in their DNA, distancing themselves with every harvest, every meal, from the patriarchal structure that brought them to the brink of disaster.

It is the best gourmet food I have ever tasted to include the ambience of the nature where tables and chairs are placed in reverence and gratitude.

I thought of the Flying Bird Goddesses in Travnik and Novi Travnik after the Balkan War. Behind the deaths of young and old women who fly from the balconies and windows of their apartment flats to avoid the continued torture, starvation, poverty, and abuse in the aftermath of the Balkan War is the misguided impulse to resurrect the Balkan Bird Goddess.

Their deaths are not listed as suicide, but as "accidental" deaths, if they are listed at all. Their wingless bodies crash many stories down to the already blood-soaked land.

Because over eighty percent of worldwide refugees are women, we must consider the impact of the economic crisis on their trauma recovery. The women of the Balkan region will not recover from the economic blow they sustained for generations.[3]

Do we even notice the crushed and broken female bodies on the ground anymore? Do we notice that there is nowhere to go? Do we wonder how they will feed their children or what privations they will face for themselves in order to do so?

Migratory birds are suffering the same fate as Balkan women. In Arkansas, red-winged blackbirds, European Starlings, common grackles, and brown-headed cowbirds fell to the ground at midnight because of large booming sounds from fireworks on January 6th, 2011.[4] According to the Serbian Orthodox religion, January 6th is the Christmas Eve when Virgin Mary labors to give birth to her son. In northwest Arkansas, the Arkansas River spewed 100,000 dead drum fish at the same time as the birds fell from the sky. Reviewing in my mind Marija Gimbutas's archeological studies of the Old Europe Bird and Fish Goddesses while attempting to grasp this phenomenon, I realized that the archaeomythology has its roots in real situations.

3 Julie Mertus, *War's Offensive against Women,* Kumarian, 2000.

4 National Geographic http://news.nationalgeographic.com/news/2011/01/110106-birds-falling-from-sky-bird-deaths-arkansas-science/

Erin Hilleary

CHAPTER 12

Bridges and Widow Goddess

WHEN AND WHERE I BORE WITNESS:

Shortly after the Mostar Bridge was restored by UNESCO in July of 2004, the Kolo Sumejja women went on a Kolo Trauma Treatment and Training retreat to the Bosnian-Herzegovina Adriatic coast. The bus route travels over the mountains and follows the Neretva River to the coast. Mostar is one of the cities that we pass through on the way to the coastal town of Neum.

The city of Mostar is famous for its bridge, which was destroyed in the Balkan war. The bridge was violently destroyed by an explosion. The old stone and wood structure collapsed into the Neretva River below requiring years of repair. The restoration process required divers and sophisticated machinery to dredge up the old stone remnants from watery graves.

In the years prior to the restoration of the Mostar Bridge, the Kolo Sumejja women and I witnessed the desolation of Mostar's shops and downtown area, bereft of their normal load of tourists. The war ensured the economic devastation of this area, but the destruction of the old bridge, which was the main tourist draw, made the situation much worse. This downturn in tourism created even greater, more long-term suffering for the people of Mostar.

Mostar Bridge & Death Divers Taken from the book The Best of Bosnia & Herzegovina, Ahmed Bosnic-Stjepan Kljuic-Goran Milic

My daughter accompanied me on this trip. She explored the ghost town of Mostar and discovered a shop full of wooden boxes and carvings. The proprietor, revived by my daughter's interest in his craft and shop, talked about his daughter, who lived in another city while he lived and slept in the shop. One of the most touching acts of the trip was the old man's gift to my daughter of one of his hand-carved boxes. The small, wooden box had all of the South Slavic icons emblazoned on it with an artistic rendering that made it imperative to study. I thought of the spiral, connecting so many things. My daughter recalled his daughter to him, while his art recalled my trauma work and my intergenerational memories to me.

The bus ride was loaded with over twelve hours of massive scenery changes and followed the spiraling Neretva River as we slowly came down from the mountains. The spiral road reminded me of the spiral icon which, like the troika (the sacred triple aspect), is the South Slavic old science, helping them make meaning out of what befalls them. One of the Kolo Sumeijja women tapped my shoulder as we passed through the mountain town called *Prozor*, which means "window." Reminding me of the town's name, she told me that it is situated just below the mountain top to facilitate the best view of the spiral of life and rivers, as it incubates the troika of Life/Death/Life. I believed her.

This troika can be understood through the lens of Coleridge's poem *The Rime of the Ancient Mariner,* in which an old man is cursed to re-tell his story to any who might benefit from his learned wisdom. At one point in his journey, he is the object of a dice game between the male Death and "the nightmare Life-in-Death," a female much like the Widow Goddess, or the witch aspect of Baba Yaga. "Life-in-Death" wins the game, plunging the mariner into a spiraling whirlpool from which he emerges "a better and wiser man." Here, the mariner escapes death, but it requires an experience of death, Life-in-Death, to make him understand the path he should be on and his relationship to all life. This mirrors the South Slavic troika of Life/Death/Life, reflecting life as an unending cycle, not a linear path with a definite end point, which allows intergenerational memories to flow from grandmother to granddaughter.

STORIED INSTRUCTIONS

I read an article about White Lake in nearby Bolotnikovo, Russia, that was fed by the Oka River. A mere 240 miles east of Moscow, White Lake drained overnight on May 27, 2005. This event was witnessed by a seventy-four-year-old resident as a spiral of water funneling into what was termed an abyss, consuming trees and fish alike right before his eyes.

The forty-eight foot deep lake filled with thirty-five pound carp was suddenly channeled into underground caverns and flowed into the Oka River. It is said the shifting soils under the lake caused the channel to form.

Near Novi Travnik, Bosnia, eighty largely unexplored caves, named "Angel" caves, are hidden by trees but have a wide road of stones leading to their entrances. The stone road was once a huge river bed, but in 1937, the river disappeared overnight. The local people knew that it was a message of coming war and Moist Mother Earth's angst. So far, their prophecy has proven accurate.

Travnik and its sister town, Novi Travnik, have many caverns of running water underneath their streets and fields. South Slavic people often discuss the oceans that they believe to be hidden inside the mountains surrounding Travnik and Novi Travnik. Sweet, ice-cold, fresh water pours from Mt. Vlasic and Mt. Vranica (Serbo-Croatian for the color brown) but neither has a glacier.

Located in the Herzegovina-Neretva Canton in the Federation, Mostar is the fifth largest city and one of the best-known and important cities in the region. The Velez Mountains surrounding Mostar are high desert with only a small, winter snowfall, an amount that is unable to account for the waters. Water is everywhere despite the region's desert-like climate. Whenever I and the Kolo Sumejja women travel to the Bosnian-Herzegovina coastal town of Neum, I always wonder where these waters come from.

One of the resting places on our journey to Neum, with the Novi Travnik Kolo Sumejja women, is a stop at the Green Waters, located at Buna just outside of Mostar. The raging green river flows from underneath a Paleolithic cave that contain a prehistoric "Green Man Mask," a traditional symbol of rebirth and regeneration. You can hear the raging river from a distance, and when you are next to the water, conversations are difficult because of the river's roar. Right next to the mouth of the cave and the outpouring of green, ice-cold waters is a Dervish Temple that does not have a roof. A simple silver cup is latched on the concrete steps going down into the river. This is where prayers are said and then, as part of the ritual, the miracle water is drunk. Slavic Thaumaturgy, with its wondering and miracle-making, is at its best here.

Buna Dervish Temple and Green Waters Taken from the book The Best of Bosnia & Herzegovina, Ahmed Bosnic-Stjepan Kljuic-Goran Milic

Shortly after our stop at the Green Waters in Buna, we would take a break in Mostar. Walking across the Mostar Bridge is rewarding for us, since the bridge's restoration took many years, especially since the pieces of the bridge had to be recovered from Neretva River. The Kolo Trauma Treatment and Training group's yearly journey to the coast would measure our own trauma recovery against the progress of the bridge restoration. I laughed at badly written English signs warning people of the bridge's dangers and read a poster in Mostar that offered a reading of Mula Mustafa Baseskija's poetry with free cigarettes and free thick Bosnian coffee for those who dared to attend. Baseskija's poetry celebrates life in the face of the great plague of 1788. He bore witness to a great calamity, and his work chronicles the past century of war in the former Yugoslavia. These are all signs of rebirth through the spiral of life and death.

Sana Koric, leader of the Kolo Sumejja, said that she would go for the cigarettes and coffee, but knew it would hook another generation into a nasty, life-threatening habit, addiction to coffee, cigarettes, and the disassociation that leads to hate. She knew that *uvreda*, her trauma and the trauma of all Bosnians, is open to all things toxic. As we know, however, *povreda,* the Bosnian word for trauma which means to injure, to push down, or infringe, also carries the meaning for worth or value. Sana refused to let the younger women see her espousing negative habits. She used her wisdom to teach others and model a better way for them to live, just like Coleridge's mariner.

Trying to quit smoking, Sana sits outside, dragging on her cigarette as she coordinates the next series of Kolo trauma training as well as the upcoming December Peaceful Dimensions Conference to remember the rape camps in Bosnia. Since March of 1999, her work and that of the Kolo: Women's Cross Cultural Collaboration has been a largely unpaid labor of a mother's love. I am aware of her clarity and vitality as it emerges into a new cycle of the spiral with her tremulous insight into *uvreda.*

Walking across the newly restored Mostar Bridge was difficult because of the uneven surfaces of the old stone. Many people crowded together as they walk across the bridge. We are unable to synchronize like the flock of birds overhead in a "V" formation. Some of the Kolo Sumejja women were eating their ice cream with relish, which slowed their pace enough so that a small space on the bridge was able to form.

I noticed a young man towering above the crowd because he was standing on the bridge's railing in his Speedo and nothing else. At first, I thought this was a suicide, but then his action registered with me: I sensed a crisis of healing, an attempt to traverse the barren aftermath of war.

His Adriatic olive-brown skin and black hair contrasted directly with the off-white stone bridge, faded from years of sun and being blown to pieces during the Balkan War sunk into the river below. The Neretva River snakes below the newly reconstructed and restoration project of the bridge, now loaded with many German and Dutch tourists.

While standing on the thick, stone rail, the diver taunted the crowd: "Fifty euros

"Are you so desperate to dive to your death for the money?"

to see me dive." I asked the young man, "Are you so desperate to dive to your death for the money?" He smiled at me.

One of the Kolo Sumejja women on the bridge told me that the young men in this area don't have a life. Another Kolo Sumejja woman demanded to know where his mother was. I had to laugh at that response, as the young man was at least twenty-five years old.

The diver turned to me and asked me if I wanted to see him dive. I then turned to the crowd forming tighter against the stone rail and asked why they would want to pay someone to do something they would not do. The crowd started to dissipate, with a few bowed heads among the bobbing tourists resembling a chaotic school of fish. Looking at the diver, I told him I would not ask where his mother was, but rather what she would do if he died for only fifty euros.

His response was a beautiful articulation of the South Slavic beliefs about rivers as incubators of the spiral of life/death/life.

Glancing at the sky and pointing to the birds and then to the river full of fish, he told me how he came to his understanding of how the birds fly and fish glide in the water. The diver spoke of the feeling of the sky against his skin once he hits the water. The water, according to him, allows him to be cleared but not necessarily cleansed, so he is driven to repeat the experience again and again. He said that diving is a habit for him, like smoking, and he remarked that his coffin would be a beautifully crafted box of spiraling birds and fish. Like Coleridge's mariner, this young man lives within Life-In-Death, constantly tracing its boundaries and testing its limits. While he does not have much of a life as we would conceive of it, he also manages to stave off death while facing it with every dive.

As I walked away, I thought of the archeological artifacts found in the former Yugoslav region, mostly decorated with the spiral and zoomorphic Bird Goddess and Fish Goddess figurines. The diver jumped down from the railing and, taking my elbow, led the way to his *chef* (meaning his boss or supervisor). Balding and wide-bodied, the *chef* spoke of the Olympian diving ability of the young men in this region, recalling that, for many generations, divers have traced a luminous bridge in the sky like a bird diving into the Neretva River below. The result is zest for being in the moment and diving into the future with new meaning.

Offering me coffee, the *chef* asked which of the inevitable deaths I would choose for this young man. Should he merge with the Moist Mother Earth, challenging himself and Life itself with each dive, or would it be better to follow his national allegiance blindly onto a battlefield, facing extermination by the weapons of war?

He smiled at me.

His question startled me, both in its stark reality and its acceptance of the inevitability of death, even for the young. His strange economics of life and death focused on finding the most meaningful way to die. This value, the value of the spiral and the troika, are discussed in my many years of Kolo trauma treatment and training.

I ask myself about the economics of maternal fright, in which infants are born with the memory of war and violence. As in many places of the world, like China, India, and Iran, South Slavic mothers are only worthy if they have sons. I asked the *chef* if the sons know that their value is to die fighting, killing in order to protect. If they survive, their lives are still not their own. They must provide monetarily for the family, even if it means death. These sons are the first to give up their lives, whether in war or its aftermath.

THE IMPACT

Mostar's *uvreda* is found in their Death Divers.

Doing a death leap for fifty euros is the economic index of what a Bosnian-Herzegovina male Muslim is worth in the aftermath of a bloody Balkan war. The economic disparity between Muslims and their neighbors is evident, and United Nations research based on twenty-four Muslim countries note levels of high poverty and birth rate as a result. [1]

Comparing wounds makes no sense. No one group has a trump card to play as the most wounded or traumatized. All were tragically impacted by the Balkan Wars and many choose to continue the hatred that fueled that war and destroyed so many lives and livelihoods.

One can only estimate what the worth is for females and children in the aftermath of war, particularly in the face of a burgeoning sex slave industry and the demand for cheap labor by corporations.

After three raging wars on Balkan soil, the ancient South Slavic way of life is slowly re-emerging for many people, as it has, for thousands of years, been reenacted and woven into the fabric of their being. Their South Slavic way of life, with its inclusion of the body in the life of all Mother Earth, heals *uvreda*. I am not sure how we can go about healing the wounds on the Bosnian spiritual landscape from the one million landmines that remain hidden there.

The somatic (living body) South Slavic way of life connects what is buried to what helps it emerge. Just as they look to the hidden oceans under the mountains, the South Slavs understand that seeds need the sun just as humans need insight. Their photism (having to do with light) is more than a connection to the earth. It is an understanding of the spirituality of the landscape, that which is hidden beneath the soil and the flesh, waiting to be released to grow in the light.

I have gained tremendous insight from watching the South Slavic approach to the hidden life within both Earth and her children. I have gained a "felt sense" of the South Slavic way of life and their oral memory traditions. My "felt sense" becomes the healing fulfillment of the changes that many have prayed for desperately.

This connects to the Bird Goddess archeological remains. According to

1 http://pewforum.org/future-of-the-global-muslim-population-related-factors-economic.aspx

archeologist Marija Gimbutas, the Bird Goddess's dual nature is "giver of life, well-being, and nourishment. On the other hand, she appears as Death in the guise of a vulture, owl, or other bird of prey or carrion eater." The Fish Goddess holds dominion over death, and "death and regeneration are expressed as interdependent, contiguous aspects of one deity." [2]

The three most important things to understand about trauma are it is something that has never happened to you before, it is a powerful agency of change occurring in potentially highly averse and violent events, and that trauma is intensified learning that includes soma (living bodies), not only in physical terms but our emotional and spiritual natures.

Trauma itself is a journey, a flight like that of the birds or the progress of a swimming fish, both feel the sky or the water on their bodies, constantly bringing change and healing.

The journey from Novi Travnik along the Neretva River allows me to focus on the insight that healing starts within each individual when fully felt emotional and feeling experiences are involved. The reciprocal side of this insight means that each individual's small acts are a co-created process that ripples across the globe.

Nothing occurs in isolation, and no one lives or dies without affecting the globe.

---

2 Marija Gimbutas, *The Civilization of the Goddess: the World of Old Europe,* (HarperSanFrancisco, 1991)

Erin Hilleary

Found in the former Yugoslav region armless women artifacts Vinca Period

CHAPTER 13

Ashes and the Poetic College

WHERE AND WHEN I BORE WITNESS:

The Poetic Colleges took place from March, 1999, to July, 2006, in Novi Travnik, Bosnia-Herzegovina. In the ashes of synchronicity, the memorial for the Ahmica-Vitez war crimes fell on the same day as the Catholic Easter in April 2006. Within the Catholic rites hides the more ancient practice of celebrating the Spring Equinox, called Ash Wednesday. Catholics perform the ritual of drawing a cross on the forehead in ash as a sign of repentance and mourning, recalling the symbolic wearing of sackcloth and ashes.

The local mosque was destroyed in the Balkan War and has not been rebuilt. It stands across a small road from the Catholic Church, which suffered no apparent damage and whose Croatian parishioners committed and/or were complicit in many of the war's local atrocities.

Muslims attending the call to prayer and remembrance that morning, memorializing their lost loved ones who died in a massacre on the very land where the survivors still lived, would hear the Catholic Church bells peal as they wept for their family members. The tolling bells of those who committed the atrocities would not sound like repentance or mourning to the Muslim survivors of wartime violence but would add to their mourning, as they were unable to worship in their own mosque.

Like the million plus landmines still buried in the former Yugoslavia, this religious divide is potentially explosive. It remains hidden, as the Muslims and Catholics pray quietly across the road form one another, but the old wounds are not yet healed and the divisions that caused the war to break out, remain.

STORIED INSTRUCTIONS

It was March, 1999, ten days before the NATO bombing of the Republic of Serbia. I was living in Holland at the time, and I received a simple email from Adam, leader of Medex Mine Awareness, asking that I come to Bosnia. Adam represented a non-governmental organization, or NGO, that trained young children to survive the landmines that remained planted in the houses and ground after the war. He told me, however, that the children and their parents were traumatized after their training and needed to speak about their fears.

The old airport in Sarajevo was filled to the brim with military staff and hardware on my first visit in response to Adam's email. The email was a poorly written appeal for help in halting English, but I knew that they needed help

Her world view did not include the genocide story or how Superman

dealing with the trauma associated with the constant threat from landmines and other aftereffects of the Balkan War.

I left the email at home, knowing that if it were found, it could shut down an airport, bring out the military, and their enormous show of weapons. This type of threat contributes to coercive diplomacy, a political strategy that ultimately leads to the loss of freedom for the civilians of the threatened area.

When I landed at the new Sarajevo airport, two male Bosnians holding up a sign with my name on it appeared as I exited customs. Taking my suitcase and walking to the car, I had severe palpitations looking at the small, banged-up car with a scrawled sign posted on the door that said "Medex Mine Awareness."

The driver Almir said this way we would avoid sniper fire.

I was incredulous that I even sat in the car, let alone endured the two-hour drive to Novi Travnik. Yet, I saw that Almir's humorous but truthful approach to the situation worked. It got us both through the fear ahead of us as we drove to Novi Travnik. I realized that Almir's joking about the harsh realities of sniper fire and the difficult work of Medex Mine Awareness showed him to be an extraordinary Poetic College professor commencing class in a downtrodden, tin box of a car.

Escalating from incredulity to total disbelief, I noticed that we were in the middle of a military convoy heading down the back route to Serbia. Novi Travnik is in alpine country, a half hour from the 1984 Winter Olympics site. The highway leading there, known during the Balkan War as "Death Highway," was the very road that the military convoy needed to take. Knowing that the NATO bombs I watched being transported would soak the people and the land in ashes led me to experience a kind of falling away, a kind of death, and enter into the deadened underworld.

Adam talked about a grant that their NGO had applied for but did not get. The grant, originating from a foundation supported by Hillary Clinton, was to develop a comic book educating Bosnian children on the million or more anti-personnel mines still in their country, each of which had a shelf life of one hundred years. Adam was both confused and furious as he showed me the book. The contract had been awarded to Disney, who had used Superman to explain the dangers of death to Bosnian children. "Do you think Bosnian children even know who Superman is?" he asked.

I told him that I doubted it. As I read more of the comic book, I was stunned by its propaganda. The book advanced the fantasy that Superman was waiting to save them from danger, an American fantasy that is safe to share with children only in an environment without hidden dangers like landmines. While propaganda appears to be similar to mythology, it is instead manipulative and seductive. Children living in the aftermath of war are vulnerable to propaganda and manipulation.

as a hero from the sky actually killed children.

Intergenerational trauma barrels down on the children, most of whom were not alive during the Balkan War but see and feel their parents' fear and residual trauma. I wondered why the grant had been given to Disney and not the Bosnian NGO, which was immersed in the South Slavic way of life and culture and stood a much greater chance of successfully educating local children.

Adam believed that there was a purposeful campaign to establish the creation of the comic books away from Bosnia and that it had been successful. He and Amir explained that several children who had read the comic book and believed its propaganda had simply believed that Superman would save them. When the fantasy failed to materialize, they died in violent explosions that took them from their parents and returned instead the trauma and horror of the war the parents had believed was over.

This is the danger of propaganda as well as taking education away from the local people who understand the children who need the training. Foreigners simply could not understand how a Bosnian child, who would be unfamiliar with Superman and who wouldn't have a father to introduce his childhood fantasy appropriately, would read this comic book. This was a terrible reality for Medex Mine Awareness.

Turning to me, Adam asked me if I wanted to know what happened to the comic books and his removal campaign.

I nodded despite being hesitant to hear what was sure to be an upsetting story. Adam told me that the $500,000 grant had been given to Disney, and that, after a protest was staged, Disney simply moved the comic books to Kosovo. Again, my heart ached to see commerce privileged over children's lives.

I returned to Holland with this story and the children's reality tucked under my heart.

I encountered the US Ambassador to Holland on the soccer field at the ex-pat school where my daughter was practicing. In the cold air of a Dutch fall, standing in crunchy grass that spoke of ice during the night before, was a dark-haired, professional woman who bragged that she would speak to President and Mrs. Clinton that very night.

I could not believe her attitude. She was missing the vitally important role that could have been fulfilling. The Poetic College remained opposed to this perspective, and I could only imagine the ashes of mourning that would cover Bosnia yet again. I couldn't escape the ashes or the intensified learning that happens when I listen openly to others' stories.

Unlike anything I have ever known, Bosnian war stories do not collapse into an amorphous mass. There is a weight to the first person narratives, the storied instructions exposing the cosmic order leading me step-by-step to situations or persons that I would never ordinarily encounter.

Somehow, my kolo trauma work and Medex Mine Awareness story circulated in the ex-pat Dutch community, reaching the ears of the ambassadress. I retold the poignant stories to her and I kept experiencing this sense from her that I was doing something wrong or not conforming to her worldview.

Her world view did not include the genocide story or how Superman as a hero from the sky actually killed children.

Grandmother in a Bosnian Graveyard

Tell me how do I tell the stories?

It was Friday, April 16, 1993, at 5:30 AM, when Croatian forces simultaneously attacked Vitez, Stari Vitez, Ahmica, Nadioci, Šantici, Pirici, Novaci, Putiš, and Donja Veceriska. All the Croats living in the same villages were warned of what was to come and the Croat women and children were evacuated in the night. Shelling of the Muslim part of Ahmica killed women, children, and the elderly. Ahmica's two mosques buckled under the extreme shelling and fire. The youngest to die was machine-gunned in his crib and the oldest was a ninety-six old woman.[1] Other bodies were found in their homes. The people had been so badly charred they could not be identified, and they lay in positions suggesting that they had been burned alive. The majority of the victims were women and children.

1 http://www.bosniafacts.info/web/ahmici_massacre.php The Ahmići massacre was the culmination of the Lašva Valley ethnic cleansing committed by the Croatian Community of Herzeg-Bosnia's political and military leadership on Bosnian Muslim (Bosniak) civilians during the Bosnian War in April 1993. It is the biggest massacre committed during the conflict between Croats and the Bosnian government (dominated by Bosniaks). The International Criminal Tribunal for the former Yugoslavia in The Hague has ruled that these crimes amounted to crimes against humanity in numerous verdicts against Croat political and military leaders and soldiers, most notably Dario Kordić, political leader of Croats in Central Bosnia who got 25 years in prison

An observer said that he had seen the bodies of children whose positions suggested that they died in agony in the flames. He reported that "some of the houses were absolute scenes of horror, because not only were the people dead, but there were those who were burned and obviously some had been burned with flame launchers, which had charred the bodies. This was the case with several of the bodies."[2]

The mute Ahmica-Vitez church and its pealing bells are meant to signify and share love and compassion. I realized instead that the bells were a metal and concrete bystander to South Slavic nationalism and patristic domination. Not unlike the ambassadress's concrete worldview.

When I went to take a picture of the concrete church and its neon cross, I was accosted and interrogated by a stocky, wide-faced Croat. He immediately calmed down when he heard my old Slavic first name, Danica, and believed that I was Croat. I said nothing but took my digital picture. I call it the "Sins of Silence," as it represents the chilling bystander syndrome found in turning the other cheek.

I am complicit and participate in the same sins of silence by using my old Slavic name that clearly is not Muslim.

2 a b "ICTY: Blaškic verdict - B. The municipality of Vitez - 1. Ahmici, Šantici, Pirici, Nadioci - b) An attack against the Muslim civilian population - iv) Murders of civilians".

It provides cover for me to travel in Bosnia and perform important trauma healing work, but it also allows me to hide from sharing the trauma of the Muslim women and children who faced such horror.

The Croat Church directly faced the Muslim memorial ceremony across the road. The newly erected neon cross blazed at the mourners as they wept. It is as if the Croats allowed their neon cross to stand as a border to fend off the violent images that were being relived only a short stroll across the street from the Croat enclave to the Muslim side of the village.

But I already know from my research into the far past that the new neon cross is far from its Paleolithic origins as a crossroad or intersection, the actual geocentric reference point in the middle of a thick forest. Not many know the story, the origins of the cross.

An uneasy silence hangs thick, the same consistency as life-smothering volcanic ashes, between the two different religious and ethnic enclaves.

The Croats attending Easter services used their umbrellas to shield their view of the Muslim enclave, tears were absent from their faces. Nor did I see ashes tumble down from the grey, brooding skies overhead. I have witnessed the phenomenon of rain occurring on one side of the street, the other side being completely dry. But the sins of silence and participation in the bystander effect were obvious in the umbrellas that day.

While the Croats used theirs to hide, so did the Muslims, whose umbrellas provided shade from complicity and hatred. The South Slavic Hard Rain, the ashes of the remains of their lives, fell on the day of the Ahmica war memorial services. Perhaps this rain was nature's way of joining in mourning with every Bosnian living in the haunted, war-scarred landscape, regardless of religion or ethnicity.

Most, I realized, do not know how to deal with invisibility but become blind to life.

^ **Standing in ruins, a pech- oven**

The bystander effect and sins of silence allow them the bliss of being blind, the bliss of "I didn't know," "I didn't do that, someone else did." They can keep pretending they are separate from the whole, the same way the Croat women and children across the road from Ahmica-Vitez Croats were evacuated on the eve of April 16, 1993, the sign of the cross on their doors. As long as we pretend that there really is an "us" and a "them," we will remain in a state of war, whether literal or figurative.

THE IMPACT:

I realized that I walked past and even talked to many Bosnians who were trapped in the lethal cast made of the ashes called "trauma" or "Post Traumatic Stress Disorder." I am usually talking to a shell of ashes.

The fairy tale of Cinderella originated in the Balkans, where she is called *Papalluga.* Slavs revere ashes, which is highlighted in many archeological remains of the *pechs* or stoves, used in "Old Europe." Often ashes were contained near the *pech* alongside Goddess figurines; however, the blasting fires of genocide and gynocide incinerated many women, often in houses burnt to the ground.

My encounters with South Slavic women war and war crimes survivors immersed my trauma expertise in a fuller and more painful training and intensified learning that does not inoculate anyone against trauma. Instead of an easy remedy, we seek the cure that comes from creating social memory by bearing witness to the holocaustic first person stories of their lives and dancing the kolo after a home-grown meal.

The ashes from a century of wars were supplanted once again by the ashes of their roasted lambs or the clearing of fields by burning brush, which sweetens the soil. Like Cinderella, the women shed their ash-covered clothing for a time and danced in health and happiness. These are true "Blood and Honey" reconstructed memories.

It was never my plan or intention to form a non-profit. In fact, I had no clue that I would be traveling for over a decade to Bosnia, Africa, Afghanistan, Haiti, India and Sri Lanka working with catastrophic trauma issues. I am continually being swept away by the ashes raining from the skies and tumbling down to Moist Mother Earth.

The mysterious progression of bearing witness to storied instructions represents the cosmic order. When we relentlessly, openly explore the world as we know it, we can learn from each other's experiences, and our own lives become part of the lives of others.

The shunning of the feminine in all Her aspects has been an ongoing war for over five thousand years, which we see in the artifacts that herald the beginning of this raging violence in ancient eras. I keep asking myself why there is so much hatred toward females. I never ask why women hate men, but shouldn't this be so with all the violence and deaths?

Both sides must be open both to examining and to examination.

Erin Hilleary

CHAPTER 14

Jerisavlja, The Female Dragon

SOUTH SLAVIC QUEEN OF FAERIES-FOREST WITCH

When and where I bore witness. From March 1999 to the present, in Novi Travnik, Bosnia, I have met many survivors. The towns, cities, and the rural communities have faces that describe the depth of wars and violence. Mostar and Pocejteli, both artists' communities are utterly breathtaking despite the war scarred buildings and homes. Both communities are about an hour or more from the Adriatic Sea. Along with Sarajevo, the windowless bombed out buildings have trees growing in its ruins. The trees are substantial and have been growing in the dismembered homes and structures for well over ten years in the aftermath of the Balkan War.

It is as if the Slavic Baba Yaga (Mother Nature) threw seeds down in the most destroyed ruins so that Mother Nature can heal the wounds of violence and wars. Within those trees now growing throughout the destroyed and torn structures are tree rings recording the violence and the war. But, with all the destruction and brutality present in the structures, the trees, twisting vines and masses of weeds erupting in every crevasse is a sign of continuance. Despite the structures' outlaw memorial to those dead, dying, and victims of violence, it outwaits, outruns and has outwitted the wars' weaponry with life.

This one interview took place in a darkened apartment. She could not help but be exquisitely sensitive to the paradoxical both/and quality of her present condition and her past. Her life experiences shape and communicate her content just as the war scarred ruins dialogue constantly with its blasted cement structures of entombment. She is a rape survivor who refuses to leave her apartment.

STORIED INSTRUCTIONS

The Kolo Sumejja women refer me to those who have need of a third party. The third party is often someone who does not live in their community and can bear witness. According to these wise women, I qualify. Relentlessly, they ask me to come visit her. But I am not given any specifics from the women. Each one tells me they learned from my trauma intensive training to not gossip. I retort back to the women, "You still gossip and do not know the difference of true sharing and confidentiality." They glare at me. I do as they ask in the end because they are truly my professors in a hard curriculum of trauma.

I am taken to her apartment building going through many twists and turns. My companions silently without my consent disappear as I trudge up five flights of stairs. Like most buildings on the Muslim side, the elevator shafts were

Novi Travnik Apartment Flats

bombed and never repaired. What this meant was the elderly living on higher floors would somehow have to carry food and firewood. If they were ill or unable, many would freeze to death or starve.

Friends and neighbors are no longer a viable way of life with the Balkan War still so fresh in the South Slavic psyche. I thought of this as I climbed the endless set of darkened steps. I was sweating wearing a warm coat, but I have no other bags to carry up the stairs. It is arduous climbing. And as I trudged upward, I turned to the broader implications of the annihilation of the South Slavic intangible heritage and practices for friendship and neighbors (prijateljstvo & susjedi). It runs contrary to the Bosnians suffering in the aftermath of wars in their daily experiences that literally hinges on life and death choices.

Of course, I am not told which door she is living behind. The women told me that since I have no sense of direction, I will know which door. I tell them this is seriously unfair, and they respond with how I have a reliable measure of knowing, intuitiveness noted in my trauma work that is in the end, the only set of directions I needed. If I say how crazy that logic is, they respond with "don't be crazy" (nemojte biti ludi!).

I end up thinking as I trudged on, "Will I be chased away when I knock at the wrong door?" Or worse yet, the stockpiles of weapons former soldiers have stored began to set up an automatic and unpleasant dialogue in my mind. I tell the Kolo Sumejja women what possibilities could transpire. Of course, the women laugh until tears spill down their blouses effectively snatching away my negativity. One of the women quipped, "You'll knock on the right door. There are no wrong doors." I swear up a storm in Bosnian, which only made my companions convulse in serious laughter.

The Kolo Sumejja women, female dragons, as usual ended up being right.

I knocked on her door, the first time, among many doors dressed in the same deranged and derelict depressing color of neither black nor brown. The women were instructing me to accept my own wildness with my lack of direction into a perspective. I learned to not forsake my intuitiveness or disclaim it. Learning from them, meant five flights of stairs and a series of doors all exactly the same chorus of dark pallor sentiments. It was left up to me to discover who is behind them, and why she is behind her door. I make a reminder to tell the women to be more direct.

Over the years of my practice across the planet in the catastrophic arenas of violence, it becomes apparent that the depth of our life experiences is behind every thought or door and becomes our immediate condition. The reality is that the untouchable past continuously impinges on our present. I saw that with the trees rising up out shelled buildings, and I saw this in the five flights of stairs and endless doors all looking like the other.

I knock on one of the doors. She opens the door within a few moments as if she was waiting for me to finish climbing the stairs. Young, just touching thirty, she places her hand to her throat and surveys the hallway directly behind me nervously. I tell her the women are not that foolish to climb five flights of stairs. She looks at me with a frightened mask and after a moment named the two women. She was accurate, and I asked her if the women arranged for my visit. She nodded no as she ushered me into the dark apartment. The female solidarity is so heightened, that the Kolo Sumejja women and this young woman have no need for words. This pushed me into a critical faculty to explore uncharted territory in western sciences but always omnipresent indigenously in women.

The apartment is tiny but spotlessly clean. I noticed no plants in her home and that the tiny balcony had not a single covered pot from which to grow vegetables. I seriously doubted that anything could grow in the dark. But beyond the windows in her flat, I could see the tree tops swaying, some with buds. I thought the bleed-through that at times surfaces from the collective level is always present despite being unaware. The possible confluences of currents that the Kolo Sumejja women, grandmothers and mothers, in their 'gossip' are but the language of the Moist Mother Earth. I knew that the Kolo Sumejja women talked with her mother to congregate a mass sentiment for life.

She was a young adult Bosnian Muslim very pretty but thin, like a sliver of wood. Beyond pale skin, her skin sang about the self-enforced entombment for the past five months in her apartment. I looked into her eyes and saw how depression ringed dark lines marked the orbs of her iris as if it was a tree ring.

Mute, but large eyes scoping out everything, she said to me immediately, "They live here too." She pointed outside to her window. It was not to the trees but to the streets below.

I respond, "Across the street, over there." She delicately nods yes.

I had gotten use to the "land of they." Relentlessly, I would tackle the land of 'they' in the kolo trauma trainings. The gnashing of teeth and cries from the women when they realized that 'they' are their fathers, brothers, uncles, and sons as well as everyone else's male relatives who commit the unspeakable. The confrontation slowly frees us to not blindly repeat the patterns of the past.

Without knowing the specifics of her situation or having any direction from the women, I ask her when the last time she left the apartment was. Her mouth gaped open in disbelief. Asking me how I knew that, she sacrifices a painful announcement: five months. I respond, like the five flights of stairs. I ask her does she make her mother climb the five flights of stairs. Hanging her head, she nods yes.

But I knew that even if her mother refused to do so, she would be happy to die. I sensed her timing was off in that it went against her nature. She forgot when it was time for life and when the time is to die. Instead of being happy to die, or the high-pitched screams that one is not ready for death, there was none of the sense of letting what must die, die.

I went directly out on the small balcony scooping up a hand full of dried leaves coiled in the corners next to the wall. Carrying the leaves to the kitchen, she protests my dragging in debris. I light a match for the stove placing the dried leaves on the counter. I tell her that I know she will not do this outside, so let's do it here.

No book or certain clinical experience would allow her to understand something that could not previously be understood. In the kitchen, I began the archeomythology from our grandmothers about the umbilical cord that is present at birth and present each time a female is penetrated psychically and physically by her partners both of her choice making and those not of her choice making. I make a point of stating that for every sexual act, it means nine years of being attached to the person unless the umbilical cord is burned away. She was stunned but intrigued.

I tell her that by conjuring up the memory of the sexual act even without talking, to a point of vividness that you can almost feel the act, is all that is needed to commence burning the leaves. I end by stating once this occurs the umbilical cord is burned away so is the tie that binds her to a life that has her encased in a living tomb.

She looks directly at me and asks me to leave but stand outside by the kitchen door. She closes the kitchen door. I hear her pounding on the table but no sound from her. I hear terrible clanging of pots and eventually, I hear ceramic dishes pitched outside the kitchen window plunging to the pavement below. I still do not enter, but silently pray that my intuition to promote a guiding confidence for her since I knew my window of healing trauma is but, perhaps, this one encounter, did not assault anyone on the ground below.

I thought, I am crazy (Ja sam luda) just like the Kolo Sumejja thought.

I was sitting on the floor next to the kitchen door, grateful for my tea thermos with the steeped Macina Trava (Nepetae catariae herba- the leaves and flowering tops of Moench) brewed at Sana Koric's house. It seemed like hours before she opened the door. She hugged me wordlessly.

How do mothers

She walked me down the five flights of stairs holding my hand. Once at the ground floor, we walked to where her dishes fell. It was on and next to the towering wood pile. She scooped up what she could and pitched it in the street gutter. She turns to me and says this is where they belong and these are my streets and home. Walking away from me she tells me to inform the Kolo Sumejja women to tell her mother that she will be coming by.

I asked her mother about her daughter. The mother sang silent heavy tears making up for the absence of her words. The mother pointed to her apartment window on the war torn street. Rape and torture among the Bosnian Muslim grandmothers, mothers, and daughters is never spoken. Nagging within me as she pointed to her daughter's window was this sense that she was talking about her rape or rapes that might have occurred. Her pain as a mother is but my pain as a mother. How do mothers and grandmothers live with this?

THE IMPACT

Finally, rape is a war crime. Yet, I need to ask what good is it when my work takes me to the Congo where mass rapes are a daily occurrence while the rest of the world watches with unsuitable voyeurism. Or to Sri Lanka? India? And throughout Africa? But what of the staggering catastrophic statistics in the USA?

I looked to planting a seed in the house of the ruined women. It is all that I have as a non-profit with no funding since it is in the forsaken arena: for women and children. I am often alone in this work. Intuition feeds me the direction in the unknown landscapes of horrific trauma. Without the seeds to plant the trees, without dignity for women and those who suffer, it atrophies into victimhood that is intergenerational. Are we doomed to repeat?

It's about taking back my female words, some of which are the current 'F' words like feminist. Taking back my South Slavic heritage and practices that ring so clearly as talismans of what is felt but for many unable to see. This required me to be brave, to be courageous, when all I wanted to do was to run from not embrace, the global wounding towards all things feminine, children, and families.

and grandmothers live with this?

Connie Simpson
Neolithic artifact

CHAPTER 15

Salutogenesis; Promotion of life that enable individuals, groups or societies to improve our world. Origins of Health

WHEN AND WHERE I BORE WITNESS.

I lived in Holland for two years under visa conditions that the spouse cannot work. But, I ended up working. I provided trauma presentations, wrote a column for the Ex-Patriot community monthly magazine, and was court-listed in Holland to work on trauma issues with Mostar Refugees.

By March 1999 I was on my first trip to Bosnia prompted by an email from a Bosnian NGO Medex Mine Awareness. The authors of the email despite the misspellings, communicated substance. What I read and comprehended in their email sufficiently pressed me to learn if we are transferring trauma, fears and problems to the future. But what led up to the journey to Bosnia started with a first person story while in Holland, not the email from Bosnia.

It was during the winter in Holland 1998, when I crossed a threshold at a Western University adjunct faculty professor's apartment in Den Hague. That threshold was not the door and entrance to the Den Hague apartment. Just as in Mother Nature's process to carry forward the life experience of the individual into the greater whole, crossing the threshold meant an expanded understanding of female's existence in an epoch of violence.

A young twenty-something former student of the professor asked her professor, who was my friend, to arrange a meeting with me. The adjunct professor, a tall Russian woman with a large voice matching her depth of kindness, breathlessly invited me specifically, to meet a young student that became her friend.

The ground floor tiny Den Hague apartment had a French door to a small enclosed garden. What looked like a dancing fluffy small towel was a lively Bischon flying through the apartment door to greet me. The aromatic food cooked by the gourmet chef, the Russian professor, whiffed beyond the apartment and into the hallway.

A short time later, a tall thin blond woman entered the apartment. Her deportment was with elegance in handling her ever constant anxiety. Unsure of her, how elegance and anxiety were partners in her orchestrated graceful demeanor, incited my thirst for understanding how someone so young had ages of experience. It was at that very moment, the adjunct professor introduced us stating that this was the primary reason for the gathering.

STORIED INSTRUCTIONS

For purposes of confidentiality, I am naming her 'Dragica'.

Dragica immediately hugged me as soon as she entered the apartment. Warmly speaking Serbo-Croatian, Dragica

I arrived from the war.

excitedly spoke of her excitement to meet me. The professor's dog was joyfully busy barking at all the extra guests in the apartment. The din of conversations and barking dog only served to reserve the space and place to speak her story.

Our plates of food on the coffee table were eaten leisurely as Dragica began haltingly. First, it was a series of questions of what I do, mostly on trauma and our South Slavic culture. Responding with only a brief description, I put to her an open ended question, 'Why do you ask?'

As I sat back on the sofa with my plate in my lap, Dragica flowed with her narrative. Not an ounce of non-stop words or superficial idioms in her unanticipated and unpredicted first person story; rather, the words and her non-verbal communications spoke for her and through her. Sprinkled throughout the dialogue, I heard my mother tongue interspered with succinct English prosaic prose.

"I arrived in the summer of 1995," said Dragica. I asked, "Arrived from where?" Dragica looked at me directly and said, "I arrived from the war." While most Slavs would hone in if she was Muslim, Serb, Dragica is Croatian. That's the thing about labeling peoples and ethnic groups. We end up not realizing that we are all connected. For instance, the victims are all South Slavs, mostly females, surviving the Balkan War. But the reality, it is all females- you and I, are all of us.

Dragica stated she was helped in November 1995. She noted the shadow of confusion across my body.

"I was saved by an American, military intelligence officer and former Legionnaire." Dragica went on to tell of a courageous escape in a Dutch pharmacy. Stunned at finally catching up to what she was saying, I had a sharp moment of insight. Emerging from a life of silence with her experience, I realized it was not just her courageous escape, but the rebirth to speech when the victim can liberate the striking and vivid narrative, a vital function of expressing what is not allowed to be said.

Dutch pharmacies similar to the United States, Walgreens or Rite-Aid stores, seemed at first to be the wrong location for the drama of her sex slavery incarceration. I was struggling with my own shock. This is Holland, this young woman is intelligent, her kindness and her blonde hair, blue eyes and stature did not fit the image of sex slaves.

I looked around my surroundings, books flowed everywhere, and delicious food was displayed in beautiful dishes. I was warm in the apartment, not suffering the cold Dutch Winter. Guilt crept

"I was saved by an American, military intelligence officer and former Legionnaire."

What has happened to her has already happened to you and me.

across my body and invaded my heart; I felt my crushing blindness.

"I thought he liked me," said Dragica. She looked down at her hands in her lap.

"It was three months we saw each other," pausing between sentences with her narrative spoke more loudly than her soft whisperings. Dragica told me how he planned a holiday in Italy. She never got to Italy. The sex slavery ring had already known it would be Holland. In Holland, with their sex industry touted as modern and natural makes it the perfect place for sex slavery to co-exist.

Sex slavery is invisible in Holland. The Dutch refer to the pimps as lover boys.

"I was never left alone," she said. Dragica added it was a group of old Jugoslav men who ran the sex slavery ring. Being so young, not even in her twenties, meant the old Jugoslav men were in their thirties and older.

I wondered if I was in the same Dutch pharmacy while she was in there. Were there others in the Dutch Pharmacy that did not notice her? How can one miss the American Intelligence Officer or former legionnaire which led her out the back door into a back street where she ran into her freedom? For that matter, what is the difference between the main street pharmacies to the back door street?

It's twelve years later, when I hear from Dragica through social media. I finished my book but felt this pull to wait a

Central Pharmacy Holland by Wessel Crikel

But, we are already the victim.

bit longer. I knew why after she contacted me and why my book waited for her. The book with its alphabet, I name as letters of trees, are filled with sagas with notable female social intelligences and female social collective.

She lives in a land far away, now. Her life is so different from the war and the sex slavery. Dragica wrote how difficult sex slavery trafficking is to halt. What she is telling us is that it started for her and many other young women about dating and then baiting the young women with their threats of leaving them. With the war emblazoned with their grief and loss of so many loved ones, their vulnerability is intense and a delicacy for the male human traffickers. Dragica went on to tell me that the next step is their aggressiveness. The men become violent.

Taking their violence, slurs against their gender is to have the victim herself see it as insults to the property they own which was Dragica in this situation. "You are used up while you live unless you escape or try, even if it meant I could die in any escape I did."

Twelve years later, Dragica did not cry in her narrative to me. Instead, her multi-tiered sense of self is stretched to express the various levels within our moment to moment experience through her authoring her first person story. Dragica communicates a transparent reality that I and others can no longer hide from. What has happened to her has already happened to you and me.

I asked Dragica to write her an overview of her story and send it to me so I can place it at the end of this book. Finally after a long delay, she writes me a message.

"I tried over and over to write and tell and retell the story, but I could not. I realized in doing this and contacting you despite the years that passed from my telling you what happened to me is that I am healing. I am no longer that pain or that victim. My story does need to be told. I've done that with you years ago, and now it is your responsibility."

THE IMPACT

I had to ask myself how many conversations have I heard with the promise to realize the truth. Scary are those conversations when what was brutally destroyed, used up will always remain so. I know it is in the cycling experience of separation and loss that drums up the fear. We need to move through the fear. Facing loss, feeling the painful bearing witness and termination of witnessing repeats and reenacts a repossession making a difference.

Any conversations about sexual violence and debates about consent need to include the barely registered on a global agenda, the brutality meted out to women and children. Purely steeped in power differences, communication, and consequences, we are faced with conversations that aren't simple.

We know that consent and sexual violence is demanded to be reduced to a yes/no polarization that freezes women into their victimhood.

One example I can give is when I sat in the 'NOW' program in Olympia, Washington with speakers discussing human trafficking. I am always irked at how language molests and dresses up the words to evade the reality of violence. I mean, why call it 'Human Trafficking, when statistically, it is well over 97% percent impacting females and children.

The patristic norm is to neutralize our gender to erase it, molest it, murder it, and commit gynocide.

And it is usually, females who in their crushing blindness and denial, who perpetuate the norm and the molesting language. At the NOW (National Organization of Women) meeting, one older female rose from her chair having an air of superiority about her and after hearing the sexual violence numbers and horrific stories from females that endured the malignancy of our world. Her frozen gray and white coiffed hair never moved while she was shaking her head when she asked if women are pimps too.

The speaker said yes, a small percentage, however, it was not by choice but survival.

I intentionally use gendered, hetero-normative labels in an attempt to keep the conversation within the patriarchal social norms we (women and children) exist in. We repeatedly do a disservice on sexual violence issues and demand to be gender-neutral. Women become martyrs and according to Jungian Analyst James Hillman, martyrs have a secret wish to be superior.

But it is at the expense of the female. Victimizing the female to perpetuate violence against her own sex, to disdain and to disown her and our gender is done to avoid being the next victim. But, we are already the victim. And women are complicit in the violence when we erase our sex, demand gender-neutrality, and prefer being the martyr. The crushing blindness cannot avoid victimhood. Rather crushing blindness is victimhood.

Too often when I speak about the violence against women, it's not about being a man-hater; it's about facing reality, and the politically incorrect but horrifically accurate statistics that males are the perpetrators. How can we evolve from the patriarchal cults and societies when we blame the victims or any female who dares to speak about the reality of her existence?

What does not make sense and injures to the point of fatally wounding children, females, and minorities is to conclude that when patriarchal male entitled and dominated societies are erased that it will be dominated by women over males. A mother cannot hate her son but is indoctrinated to disdain and erase her daughter's sex. Rather, a mother does not rule over any sentient being.

Evolutionary Biologist Chris Knight in his thesis arrived at the conclusion that violence against females began when females stopped menstruating together.[1] He observes how every menstruating female is gathered away from the males into what he termed as 'a natural sex strike'. At that point, females had the power and empowerment. I am curious to know what would be the female global response not performed through patriarchal structures?

Imagine the impact of a global sex strike where men who have the position and power to halt the sexual violence will be compelled to act humanely and responsibly. This natural sex strike configuration based on female's biological process, literally means when we bleed together, we have female solidarity. However, the bleeding from wounds, gynocide, and sex slavery has taken over and females bleed together not

1 Chris Knight, (1991). Blood Relations and the Origins of Culture. (Yale University Press, London) pp. 24 and 25.

Amsterdam red light district

from menstruation – a natural female soma solidarity- but from hatred and mass murder towards her sex.

The event of Monkey Hill in Regent's Park Zoo WWI era in United Kingdom is chilling. Transplanting the Hamadryads baboon community in the London zoo resulted in alpha males dominating harems of females.[2] Infanticial Alpha baboon males, in the same tradition of the Greek myth depicting Chronus and his son Zeus who killed and castrated his father, went into the hands of rival baboon males. Killing by the Alpha baboon males incurred the bloody and gory killing of every female harem and their offspring.

Knowing the real truth of women's experiences is very costly. No possible reconciliation or resumption of life is found in crushing blindness.

A recent article by the Daily Mail Reporter, June 26, 2012, has a headline stating that the FBI rescued 79 teenagers in a child sex slave massive three-day prostitution sweep across the states.[3] Rescue by the FBI meant handcuffing the teenagers for the social services custody.

2 Ibid.

3 FBI rescues 79 child sex slaves in massive three-day prostitution sweep across the US. By Daily Mail Reporter PUBLISHED: 12:44 EST, 26 June 2012 | UPDATED: 16:00 EST, 26 June Read more: http://www.dailymail.co.uk/news/article-2165051/FBI-rescues-79-child-sex-slaves-hotels-truck-stops-massive-day-raid-country.html#ixzz1z0QtygGL

About the Author

A trail blazing world traveling forensic psychotherapist since 1999, Dr. Danica Anderson continues her trauma resiliency and healing psychological approach, the Kolo, the round dance and to be in a circle with women in Afghanistan, Africa, Bosnia-Herzegovina, Haiti, Sri Lanka and Kerala, India. She learned over and over again, how women forge healing collaborative communities. Dr. Anderson carries their experiences across international borders and war zones and enters into their everyday lives.

No matter the incoming mortars or her barracks blown up in Afghanistan (2013-14), or the international criminal court consultancy for war crimes-rapes in Congo DRC (2005-2014) and in the aftermath of the Haitian earthquake 2010, Anderson learned that despite the taboo of women narratives in media, rule of law to policies, their life experiences held no distortions. Women's narratives tell the stories of their invisible and neglected lives which hold the secrets of healing trauma and violence.

She has trained thousands of women, victims of violence, as lay therapists of their families thus healing their communities. Anderson has presented at numerous professional conferences worldwide, and is founder of her non-profit The Kolo: Women's Cross Cultural Collaboration, centered on roots of culture being biological; the mother and/or major caregiver.

Dr. Anderson by researching and focusing on female culture and female humanities within the oral memory science and traditions framework applies cultural applications fostering organizing social collectives vibrant with interpersonal neurobiological based resiliency skills needed for trauma recovery.

CPSIA information can be obtained at www.ICGtesting.com
Printed in the USA
BVIW12n1657310815
415357BV00001B/1